THE SINGLE PERSON'S GUIDE TO BUYING A HOME

Elaine J. Anderson, Ph.D.
Hilary W. Swinson, Contributing Editor

BETTERWAY BOOKS
CINCINNATI, OHIO

Typography by Blackhawk Typesetting

The Single Person's Guide to Buying a Home. Copyright © 1993 by Elaine J. Anderson, Ph.D. Printed and bound in the United States of America. All rights reserved. No part of this book may be reproduced in any form or by any electronic or mechanical means including information storage and retrieval systems without permission in writing from the publisher, except by a reviewer, who may quote brief passages in a review. Published by Betterway Books, an imprint of F&W Publications, Inc., 1507 Dana Avenue, Cincinnati, Ohio 45207. 1-800-289-0963. First edition.

97 96 95 94 93   5 4 3 2 1

Library of Congress Cataloging-in-Publication Data

Anderson, Elaine J.
    The single person's guide to buying a home : why to do it and how to do it / Elaine J. Anderson.
        p. cm.
    Includes bibliographical references and index.
    ISBN 1-55870-279-2 : $11.95
    1. House buying. 2. Single people—Housing. 3. Mortgage loans.   I. Title.
HD1379.A586   1993
643'.12'08652—dc20
                                                                    92-38465
                                                                    CIP

This book is dedicated to my extraordinary parents; my loving and devoted mother, Ellen, and to the memory of my caring and proud father, Lewis.

Preface

This book is not written for married couples who want to buy a home. There are many books already available for these traditional home buyers. Instead, this book is written for the single person who is ready to stop renting an apartment and buy a home. This group as a whole — single people or people who are single again — is often seen in a different light from the traditional home-buying married couple looking for a house and/or lender for a mortgage loan. The obstacles frequently experienced by the single person buying a home should not deter you from your dream to purchase a home — as long as you are ready to deal with them.

I bought my first home in a small town near my workplace. It was a ranch-style brick and stucco house, with three bedrooms, an eat-in kitchen, a dining area, and a living room featuring a floor-to-ceiling stone fireplace. It had one full bathroom, an unfinished cement-floored basement, and an attached one-car garage. The house sat on a narrow, deep lot on a hill. It was on sewer and public water service. It had oil-fired hot water baseboard heat. I remember a friend helping me paint the exterior wood trim and the stucco walls. I remember painting the walls inside the house and having carpeting installed. I remember hanging a lovely ceiling lamp over my dining room table. I remember the curtains I hung. I remember my parents coming to see my home with gifts to help fill my kitchen cabinets with pots, pans, utensils, and dishes. I remember how proud I was to put the freshly painted numbers on my mailbox with my name above them.

Although I was guided by my Realtor, I recall being somewhat overwhelmed by the financing and mortgage figures, naive about the Agreement of Sale, and intimidated by the maze of activity at settlement. I remember it as though it were yesterday. I was lucky that buying my first home turned out so well. I want you to be knowledgeable so that you can approach the often intimidating process of buying a home with confidence.

Each chapter will tell you about important aspects of buying your home. The book will provide real scenarios on home buying by single buyers, as well as samples of documents used in the purchase of a house. It will provide worksheets for you to fill out to practice your buying skills. This book is written for the novice and is technical enough to address tricky real estate questions for the single home buyer. The glossary and resources provide additional information. Enjoy!

Acknowledgments

I want to express my gratitude to everyone who in some way made this book a reality. Among those who reviewed and commented on my work as it developed, especially those who gave me permission to use bits and pieces of copyrighted material are: Bankers Systems, Inc., Minnesota; City of Harrisburg, Bureau of Codes Administration; Commonwealth Land Title Insurance Company, A Reliance Group Holding Company, Harrisburg/Philadelphia; C.M. Detweiler, Inc. Realtor, Camp Hill; Dauphin National Bank, Harrisburg; Dearborn Financial Publishing Company, Illinois; Financial Publishing Company, Boston; Greater Harrisburg Association of Realtors; Consumer Affairs Division, American Association of Retired Persons; all those who contributed their stories and ideas; and Hilary Swinson, a supportive and remarkable editor.

Most of all, I want to thank Lorraine, whose idea it was for me to put all this information in the form of a book in the first place and who has contributed valuable hours of criticism and review.

Contents

Introduction

WHY BUY A HOME?

Why would you, as a single person, want to buy a home? For some people, the reasons are obvious. In your own home, you can paint the walls lime green and the floors purple — something you are unlikely to be allowed in a rented house or apartment. Your own home is just that — a place that is only yours, to share or not, to decorate just as you like without risking the disapproval of a landlord.

But the tax and investment benefits of owning your home probably carry even more weight than the personal advantages. When you purchase a home, you will realize significant tax benefits. Discount points (usually called just "points") incurred at the initial purchase are generally tax deductible, as are many of the closing costs. Mortgage interest is deductible, and in the first few years of the loan, almost all of your monthly payment is interest, very little goes toward the principal. Property taxes (which are usually held in escrow by the mortgage company and paid once or twice a year) are deductible. For at least the first few years of the mortgage, these deductions could amount to thousands of dollars.

A home is almost always a good investment. Property values almost always go up. I say "almost always" because occasionally, in a particular locality or a particularly tough economic period, the value may hold steady or even drop. It is, however, much more likely that the value of your home will increase each year, even if you do only the minimum to maintain your home's condition. If you choose to make improvements to the home, you reap double benefits. You will be able to enjoy those improvements while you live in the home, and they will increase the home's resale value if and when you decide to sell. For instance, covering a peeling stucco exterior with new vinyl siding, which needs no painting and little maintenance, could add $5,000 to $10,000 to the value of your home.

Another advantage of buying a home is the possibility of special grants. As a single buyer, your income may be low enough to qualify you for special development or block grants. Such a grant may help with your down payment or qualify you for a loan at a lower interest rate. These grants usually have some strings attached; i.e., you may be required to guarantee not to sell the home for several years after the purchase. Call your city or county housing office to check on availability and conditions of grants.

DISADVANTAGES

Are there any disadvantages to owning your home? Sure there are, and you should definitely take them into account when deciding to purchase a home. If you buy a house, you alone are responsible for meeting the mortgage payments, paying the utility and other bills, and maintaining the home. What happens if you become ill or are laid off your job? Who will make your mortgage payments? You should plan to keep enough money in savings (or easily recoverable investments) that you can make your payments for several months even if you are out of work.

Utility and other bills can really add up, especially if you have not been responsible for them as part of rental costs. As a renter, you probably did not pay water bills or trash pickup fees directly. Even your electric and heating costs may have been included in the rent. Each of these costs may not amount to a great deal on its own, but if you add them all together you could be talking about easily $200 a month.

If you choose to live in a condominium or a subdivision, you will probably have to pay association fees monthly or quarterly. These are significant costs that should be taken into account as part of your total housing cost.

As a renter, if your water heater burst, damaging the floor beneath it, your landlord was responsible for replacing the water heater and repairing the damaged floor. As a homeowner, these costs are your responsibility. There will always be unexpected repairs and expenses incurred as part of owning a home. This is one of the best reasons to have a potential property inspected by a professional home inspector before the contract is finalized. You can avoid many potential pitfalls by using a professional inspection service to identify problem areas.

WRAP-UP

For most people, the advantages of owning a home far outweigh the disadvantages. If you are thinking of buying a home, take into consideration total housing costs, including utilities, condo or association fees, and maintenance. If you expect to make a distant move in the near future, you may want to continue renting for a while. You may have trouble making your money back if you must put the house back on the market within a year or two. A house is (almost) always a good investment, but it is certainly more likely to be so over the long term.

— 1 —

How Much House for Your Money?

Sam was very pleased with himself because he had set a goal to save $10,000 to buy a house by the time he was twenty-three, and he had managed to do it. Now he was ready to find a house to buy. He was rich! Sam had a steady job and a comfortable annual income of $25,000. His weakness was his new sports car. A major chunk of his monthly income went into car payments. The next big bill was his credit card payment. Sam felt he was ready to be a homeowner. He soon spotted the house he wanted with an asking price of $150,000. Do you think that Sam can afford this house? (Consider that his car payment is $400 and his credit card payment is $100 each month.)

Sam must understand the loan ratios used by mortgage lenders to determine whether a potential buyer qualifies for the amount of borrowed money (which translates into monthly payments) he will need to buy the house he wants. In Sam's case, whether the lender used the 25/33 or the 28/36 ratios, Sam is out of his current price range and will not qualify for the $150,000 house.

You have a certain amount of money to spend on your housing purchase. You have probably already determined an approximate amount you can afford for a down payment, and extra money will be needed for closing costs and a "cushion" in your savings or checking account. In fact, your mortgage lender will probably require proof of one to two months' mortgage payments in a bank account in order to approve your mortgage loan.

How do you determine, based on both your down payment and your projected monthly payment, how much house you will be able to afford? There are several ways to go about this; some are more effective than others.

LOAN RATIOS

Mortgage lenders use loan ratios to determine the amount of a potential mortgage. The most common ratios are 25/33 and 28/36. The ratios are based on your gross annual income (this is the first red flag you should notice). In the case of the 25/33 ratio, your gross income is multiplied by 25%. For example, if your gross income is $50,000, 25% of that figure is $12,500. To complete the first half of this calculation, this number is divided by twelve to determine a monthly payment amount of $1,042.67.

Then the 33 part of the ratio comes into play. Your gross income is multiplied by 33% and the answer divided by twelve:

$50,000 x .33 = $16,500
$16,500/12 = $1375

The $1375 figure is the maximum amount for your monthly mortgage payment plus all your long-term debt. Long-term debt is usually defined as car payments, credit card payments, and installment loan payments. For the purposes of this example, let's assume you have a $300 car payment and pay $100 a month in other long-term debts. This $400 is subtracted from $1375 to indicate the maximum mortgage amount. The two figures (based on the 25% and 33% calculations) are compared and the lower of the two is the monthly payment amount for which you are qualified; in this case, $975.

The 28/36 ratio is computed exactly the same way. Let's use the same example and plug in the figures:
$50,000 x .28 = $14,000
$14,000/12 = $1166.67
$50,000 x .36 = $18,000
$18,000/12 = $1,500
$1,500 - $400 = $1,100

Using this ratio, you would qualify for a $1,100 monthly payment.

Pitfalls of Relying on Formulas

There are some potential pitfalls to relying solely on these loan ratio formulas to determine how much house you can afford. A mortgage lender may talk a very good case for pursuing the maximum loan amount so you can buy a more expensive property. (Although the lender does not want you to default on the loan, he or she is often making money based on the total loan amount.) The formulas are based on an ideal that is rarely reached by the average consumer. The formulas do not take into account the fact that your car may break down. How will you pay for a major repair if it means you cannot make your mortgage payment?

Remember the red flag mentioned above? These loan ratios are based on your gross income — before the Internal Revenue Service and Social Security have taken their cuts, before your IRA or other plan deduction, and before you have saved any money. Do not simply assume that because a mortgage lender says you can afford a certain amount, you really can. I do not recommend that you take the amount determined by a loan ratio at face value *unless* you have no car payment, no long-term debt, no plans to incur any in the near future, and a large savings account.

Your gut reaction to a monthly payment amount is probably a better gauge than formulas. Assessing your current expenses and using them as your guide for how much you are prepared to spend is an even better method.

CURRENT EXPENSES

Prepare a list of your current expenses — how much you spend now, based on your current income. Include all the basic and essential items, but don't forget the luxuries and non-essentials as well. Start with:

Rent
Utilities (electric, water, gas, sewage, trash pickup, cable)
Car payment
Car insurance
Health insurance
Life insurance
Credit card payment(s)
Installment loan payment
Food
Clothing
Hobbies/entertainment
Educational expenses
Child support/alimony

Make as close an approximation as you can for the amount you spend in any given month. You may want to get out six months' or a year's worth of check stubs to work up this figure. Try to factor in those items you only pay sporadically as well; quarterly car insurance payments, for example. If your quarterly car insurance payment is $300, add $100 to your monthly expense list.

Now take this expense list and compare it to your monthly income. Project raises, higher commissions, and bonuses only if you are absolutely sure you will get them. It is always better to err on the side of caution. Remember, if your home is foreclosed upon, it will be at least three years before you can buy another.

Project the maximum monthly mortgage payment you believe you can afford. You must keep in mind that your mortgage payment will include not only principal and interest but a homeowner's insurance payment, property taxes, and, most likely, PMI. PMI is Private Mortgage Insurance. This is insurance the bank takes out on your loan in case you default. PMI is not designed to pay off your mortgage in the event of your death. It protects the bank or lending institution only. Most lenders require that you pay PMI unless or until you have paid off 20% of the home's equity. If you make a 20% down payment (assuming the bank's appraisal matches your offer), your lender will probably waive the PMI. Be sure and ask about this or your lender may include it anyway.

The mortgage lender always requires proof of a homeowner's insurance policy to take effect as soon as you close on a home. In addition, the lender will want to pay the policy out of funds held in escrow from your mortgage payments. That way, the lender can be sure the insurance payments are made and their investment is protected. The same is true of property taxes. Depending on the area you choose to live in and the assessed value of the home, your property taxes could be substantial.

Although these charges — PMI, homeowner's insurance, and property taxes — may not add up to a great deal per month, they could add just enough to get you out of your comfort zone.

All things considered, it is best to follow your own instincts when determining how much you can afford. If your mortgage lender insists you can afford $1000 a month, and you are uncomfortable going over $750, remember one thing. The mortgage lender is not the one writing the check to make the payment each month, you are.

QUICK CHECKLIST
HOW MUCH HOUSE FOR
YOUR MONEY?

1. Do you understand how mortgage lenders use loan ratios?
2. Have you worked out your own loan ratios?
3. Do you understand that the monthly cost the lender says you can afford may be out of your comfort zone?
4. When totalling up your current expenses, did you include both essentials and luxuries?
5. Did you roughly factor in PMI, property tax, and homeowner's insurance payments?
6. Do you know how to budget in order to protect your investment?
7. Do you know your bottom line? What you can really afford? What you are willing to spend?

— 2 —
Your Needs and Wants

Helen had lofty ideas of what her first house would be. The daughter of wealthy parents, she had grown up on a small estate. Helen began her search a few months after taking her first job in a small midwestern city. While working with a Realtor to find the home of her dreams, she became quickly disillusioned by the sample of homes she was being shown. She thought they were too small, too ordinary, and too close to the neighbors. The Realtor explained that the size houses she was seeing were within her current means. What could Helen have done to better understand the cost impact of her dream house?

Helen, like many children of successful parents, believed that a home like her parents' was available for the taking. When the features of a home like the one she grew up in are itemized, the price tag is out of reach. Helen needs to start with a house that she will like, can afford, and can sell someday for a larger home.

SEPARATING NEEDS FROM WANTS

Notice that the key word in this section is *need*. We all have a far longer list of *wants* than needs. But at this point, it may be necessary to trim down your list of "necessary" features to keep the house affordable. You may be able to add some features to your home later, depending on how handy you are in the area of home improvements.

It is unlikely that your dream house will be easy to locate. Be prepared to be flexible. Try to be realistic about what would be necessary to bring a potential house into your dream house picture. If the dream and the reality are too far apart, keep looking.

When you are looking for a home to purchase, separating your needs from your wants is an important part of the process. You may even find it helpful to pin these down before you look at a single home. Be truly discriminating in determining your needs; it is too easy for wants, or desires, to masquerade as needs. Desires are also especially good at driving prices up. That spa tub in the master bath suite looks wonderful, but is it worth the extra thousands you will pay for it? Only you can decide.

If you love to cook and entertain a great deal, certainly space for these activities is a priority for you. If you eat out a lot, you can probably make do without a separate dining room if you have an eat-in kitchen. If you have overnight guests only a couple of times a year, do you really need a guest bedroom? Maybe, if it can do double duty as a home office, exercise space, or den. Maybe not, if the price tag is too high and you can make do with a sofabed or futon. You may also want to consider the fact that three-bedroom tend to be much better in terms of resale than two-bedroom homes. (This applies to detached homes and some townhouses, not condominiums.)

Do you really want a full basement, or will a house built on a slab meet your needs? While it is possible

– 15 –

to finish an unfinished basement and gain more living space, you will probably only want to do this if: (1) the plumbing is already roughed in; (2) there is provision for heat to the basement area; (3) the basement is the walk-out type, preferably with windows. Finished basements with no windows tend to be very gloomy, and are not a good value in terms of recouping your investment upon resale of the home.

SPECIAL NEEDS

If you have special requirements, be sure to take those into account in determining your needs. If you are disabled or wheelchair-bound, a single-story home on a level lot with nearby parking is a priority for you. Barrier-free living may be a very important consideration. Even if you do not need these features now, if you plan to stay in the house a long time, you may need them in the future. It is certainly possible to add such features later, but it will be considerably more expensive than purchasing a home with them already in place. You may find *The Complete Guide to Barrier-Free Housing* by Gary D. Branson a helpful reference on this subject (Betterway, 1991).

ASK FOR THE MINIMUM, GET MUCH MORE

Try to pin down your needs in terms of *minimums*. That way, you may be pleasantly surprised to find you get more than you planned. Keep in mind, however, that if you view a particular feature as a "want" but you cannot imagine living without it, you will probably never be happy in a home that is missing that feature. For instance, if your passion is gardening — you like to pick fresh herbs for cooking, grow cut flowers for display in your home, and cultivate fresh vegetables all summer — a fifth floor condo with a tiny balcony is probably not going to make you happy.

Use the following checklists to define first your needs and then your wants.

Housing Needs

Lawn: ___ large   ___ small
Exterior:
  solid foundation
  structurally sound
  watertight roofing
Systems:
  reliable electrical system
  adequate water and sewer service
  reliable heating system
  functioning air conditioning
  good water pressure
  adequate insulation
  reliable plumbing system
  sufficient hot water supply
  no water or moisture problems
Design:
  enough living space
  minimum of _____ bedrooms
  minimum of ____ bathroom(s)
  sufficient storage/closet space
  dining area or eat-in kitchen
  sufficient cabinet and counter space

Housing Wants

Land:
  Large lot
  Attractive landscaping
Structure:
  Brick foundation
  Brick or stone construction
  Vinyl siding
  Solar features
Design:
  Energy-efficient windows/doors
  Large kitchen
  Porch or deck
  Fireplace
  Formal living room
  Formal dining room
  Additional ____ bedroom(s)
  Additional ____ bath(s) or half bath(s)
  Good floor plan
  Sufficient parking
  Other: _____

— 3 —
Location, Location, Location

Martha was a young, single, inexperienced home buyer in a small city on the East Coast. She had a good government job and was tired of renting. Martha had been in the city for a few months when she decided to buy her first house. She spotted a small row house in a marginal part of the city that everyone said was sure to be an up-and-coming neighborhood. She had not saved too much money, but had planned to look for a house in the $50,000 range. She contacted the real estate office on the "For Sale" sign and arranged to see the house. It needed work on the inside as well as the outside. The Realtor said that she could probably get the house for less than the asking price of $55,000, considering all the work it needed. Martha was delighted and offered $45,000 for the property that very day. She intended to put down $15,000 so that she would only have to borrow $30,000. She believed this would keep her monthly payments to a minimum. The owner accepted her offer and signed the agreement of sale. Martha was thrilled. Unfortunately, Martha did not find out until after settlement that houses in the area had been selling for $25,000 to $28,000. What questions did Martha forget to ask before she made her offer on this house in this location?

Martha needed to do her homework! She would have been wise to ask about the price of houses in the area. She could have asked her Realtor to prepare a list of comparables (see example) to give her a better idea of the home's value. Based on the home's condition, she would have to budget for repairs to the house. Martha

should have checked to be sure that she was not paying a highly inflated price for the property. If she pays too much for the property, it will be difficult to recover her investment in the near future. She might even have to sell at a loss if she decides to move within a few years.

CHOICES

In this beautiful country of ours, there are many choices for the location of your home as a single person. Everyone has a favorite place, a special section of the country where he or she wants to settle down. Some singles like urban living, others prefer rural areas, and still others want only to live in the suburbs. Many of us like to plant a garden, have a pet or two, mow the lawn, and rake leaves. On the other hand, some professionally employed singles are very busy during the workday and do not have time for extra upkeep at home. They prefer low maintenance and minimal chores at home in order to free up leisure time.

What does this mean when deciding on your home? Considering that you probably started out living with your parents in their home until you could manage to live on your own, it is sometimes a surprise to realize the full responsibilities of home ownership. Before this big step, you have lived alone or with friends in an apartment or maybe a house. You more than likely shared the rent and other costs of food and utilities. You may even have had chores to do. Whatever the arrangement, eventually you arrived at a time in your life that was frightening indeed. You thought about buying a home. Even though still single or single again, you go for it!

The question is, where will you want to buy your home as a single person? The location you select will be a key factor in this important first step toward buying your home.

URBAN

Cities in the United States offer both opportunities and challenges for the single person looking for a home. Many of us, because we are single, can take employment where the jobs are without the same trauma faced by families when relocating.

Large cities have much to offer: museums, nightlife, sporting events, concerts, parks and recreational areas, restaurants, and more. Smaller cities probably have many of these features, just not as many of each one.

No matter how large or small the city, it is divided into neighborhoods or sections that are well known by the residents. Some sections have names and are "the place to live in the city." It is up to you to explore and find out which section of the city offers you the style of living you want. Don't automatically decide on the area that seems to be the most trendy or popular right now. Property values (and therefore taxes) may be very high, and you would do better in a less popular neighborhood with homes that have similar features. Keep in mind that the diversity of the city is what gives it its richness and uniqueness.

Small cities (less than 500,000 population) as well as larger cities (well over a million population) offer public transportation, to assist the working population's movement to and from the workplace. If a city is for you, consider the location of the home in relation to available public transportation.

Consider, too, that it may be possible for you to bicycle or walk to work. This is especially desirable when you are also located near stores, theaters,

restaurants, and parks. Often single people find housing where they know other singles live.

Many cities offer affordable homes. Frequently, older homes in the city are large and well-built, and you get a lot for the money. On the other hand, living in posh areas of the city may be expensive yet very desirable for many.

Living in the city also provides other conveniences. The neighborhood pub; the pizza parlor with home delivery; the Chinese food takeout; the local mall food court of ethnic favorites — all are easy, quick sources of food for the active schedule of the single person.

Night life in the city frequently beckons the single person. Fashionable restaurants, nightclubs, and tea rooms make the city an inviting place to meet friends after work.

It is important to remember that you will be the homeowner in a township, borough, city, county, municipality, or some other political subdivision. You will be asked to pay taxes for services, schools, and protection. You need to know if this community is on the decline, stable, or growing. Look for telltale signs in the neighborhood to help answer these questions. For example, is the general appearance of the neighborhood well kept, free of trash and uncollected garbage? Are the homes in good repair and painted? Or is there an abundance of abandoned vehicles on the streets or in the driveways? Are there signs of unkempt houses and lawns or yards, and general lack of property care? Drive around the area and observe carefully the neighborhood at different times of the day and evening.

City life can be exciting and fulfilling while at the same time stressful. Space in the city is usually at a premium. Single houses with lawns and garages are rare in the city proper, while townhouses, condominiums, row houses, and semi-detached homes are more popular styles. As you look farther from the city center and more toward the outskirts of the city, houses standing alone with lawns and garages will be the style. If you continue moving away from the center and beyond the city limits, you will enter the residential area known as the suburbs.

Questions to Help Clarify Your Urban Choice
Use the following questions to help determine whether an urban location is right for you.

1. Does it matter how far from your workplace you live?

2. Would getting to and from work be a problem from the location you have chosen?

3. Is this location convenient to:
   ___ shopping
   ___ schools
   ___ churches
   ___ health clubs
   ___ service stations
   ___ public transportation
   ___ libraries
   ___ banks
   ___ restaurants
   ___ theaters
   ___ sports activities
   ___ parks
   ___ other places of interest to you

4. What kind of neighborhood best describes the location you have selected? Is it up and coming, stable, new, declining?

5. Talk to homeowners in the neighborhood. How do they describe the neighborhood?

6. Are there a lot of school-aged children in the neighborhood?

7. What do property taxes average in the neighborhood?
   Jot down the address of the property or properties you are considering and go to the locality's tax office. The people there can check the property address and provide this information for you.

8. Is there ample parking for you and your friends?

9. Do you feel safe as you walk in this neighborhood? Call the police department and ask about the crime rate in this area.

10. What price range are the houses selling for in this neighborhood?

11. Are there other single owners in the area?

12. Are the houses on public water and sewer or well and septic?

These questions should be helpful in identifying important considerations about an urban location for your home. Living in the city can be an exciting, communal, and enjoyable experience. Friends can easily walk to your house and drop in to visit. You can walk for pizza and soda or just develop a sense of community while sweeping your sidewalk. Some of the most pleasant times of your life can be found in the city.

SUBURBAN

Some years ago, in an effort to gain more space, families began moving to new developments on the outskirts of the city. The typical suburbanite had a three- to four-bedroom single-family house on a lot with a two-car garage.

The single person who chooses to live in the suburbs will probably commute to work by car or train. There will be a mall and large food store at a convenient distance.

Suburbanites take time and pride in their lawn care. The weekend hum of lawn mowers is the predominant noise in an otherwise usually quiet neighborhood.

Suburban life differs somewhat from city life. Space, cookouts, and riding mowers paint a different suburban picture from a grill, flower boxes, and condo fees of the city. In suburbia you can spend long undisturbed afternoons on a backyard project. Spacious lawns lend themselves to grand parties with volleyball and badminton. A quietness permeates your lifestyle. A fireplace in winter adds to the serenity of suburban living, undisturbed by neighbors a healthy distance away.

**Questions to Help Clarify Your
Suburban Choice**
The following questions will help you determine whether a suburban location is right for you.

1. Are there good train connections to your workplace?

2. Can you carpool to work?

3. Is there a park-ride station nearby?

4. Do you have a lawn mower or the money to hire a lawn service?

5. Are your neighbors far enough away for privacy?

6. Will you have the time and money to maintain the house and grounds?

7. Are the mall and food store close enough?

8. Are taxes within your budget?

9. Are sewers in or does the township plan to make that improvement in the near future? This will have an impact on your taxes.

Use these questions as a guideline to your choice to live in the suburbs.

Suburban living can be a rich experience. You can spread out, develop hobbies, get to know your neighbors in a non-intrusive way, and settle into your own quiet space.

RURAL

For some single buyers, country living is the only choice. They enjoy having lots of outdoor space. They will hear the birds, crickets, and frogs. They will see the sky sprinkled with stars on a clear night, watch the seasons change, and feel the serenity of the first snowfall. They will have acreage. They may have outbuildings, farm animals, pets, gardens, and crops.

Unless you plan to work at home or on the farm, you will commute to your workplace. When you live in the country, even something as simple as grocery shopping must be a planned event.

Winters can be especially challenging for people who live in the country. If your part of the country experiences significant snowfall, you may need a four-wheel-drive vehicle just to get out of your driveway. You may even find yourself isolated by heavy snows several times a year.

Rural property will vary from a modest couple of acres to a beautiful private estate of many acres. Access to rural property may be a surfaced road, an unfinished road, or even across someone else's property through a "right of way" agreement.

Usually, the property will be on a septic system and will have a well water supply. (Well pumps are usually powered with electricity.) Generally, such properties are heated with oil, wood, or electricity. Keep in mind that oil heat is expensive, and relying on wood heat means you will either have to buy wood to fuel a wood stove or cut the wood yourself. Electric baseboard heat can be very expensive. Heat pumps are rare except in the newest homes. The house will have electricity unless it is a remote mountain cabin so isolated that it will need to use propane gas and generators or possibly solar power for a primary or secondary energy source.

Hunters may be interested in hunting on your land for small game. You can post your land if you do not want to open it up to hunters. On the other hand, if you like to hunt, you will have the land on which to do so. Farmland is generally more expensive per acre than mountain land. Access to water, streams, ponds, and lakes is a plus.

Questions to Help Clarify Your Rural Choice
Consider the following questions to help clarify your rural location choice.

1. Do you prefer farmland or mountain land?

2. Do you want space for farm animals?

3. Do you intend to work the land? Lease it out to a farmer?

4. Do you want "modern conveniences" or a rustic lifestyle?

5. Will you live alone or have help to manage the land?

6. Are you handy? Can you fix things until help comes?

7. Will you mind commuting in bad weather?

8. Will you feel isolated?

Country living can be a challenging, peaceful, and rich experience. It offers a sense of freedom not possible anywhere else. Country living can be beautiful and expanding for people who enjoy the outdoors and do not mind long, peaceful evenings.

I once met a young man who said what he liked best about living in the country was that when he could not sleep at night, he would sit in his front yard in his pajamas at 2 a.m., listening to the crickets and looking at the stars.

HOUSE, TOWNHOUSE, OR CONDO

In considering location, you must also consider the question of house vs. townhouse vs. condo. When many people think of buying a home, they think only of a traditional house: four walls, front and back doors, a yard, etc. But for some people, a house may not be the most practical option.

A house requires a lot of upkeep, on the house itself as well as on the yard. Obviously, if you have grass to cut you will need a lawn mower. If you have shrubs, they will need to be trimmed and maintained; trees may require pruning or raking in the fall. The home's exterior will require regular (sometimes frequent) maintenance. If the siding is painted, it will need to be repainted every five to seven years. Brick, stone, vinyl, and aluminum siding generally require little maintenance, but the trim around windows and doors will certainly have to be kept up.

A townhouse, on the other hand, will probably need less exterior maintenance. The neighborhood may hire a landscaping contractor to take care of grass cutting, raking, and the like. The contractor would generally be paid out of the association fees you pay monthly or quarterly. You will still be personally responsible for the exterior of the home, including the roof. In addition, you may be very limited in the choices of exterior treatments the association allows. Some associations go so far as to provide a specific list of allowable paint colors.

For many people, especially those in big cities, a condominium is the only option. A condo provides the convenience and low maintenance costs of an apartment with the pride of ownership of a house. Your condo association fees will be used to pay for maintenance of the building's exterior and common areas, such as stairways, lobby, and garage or parking area. You will still be responsible for maintaining the interior of your living space, including

its appliances and, in the more modern buildings, heat pump or other heating/cooling devices.

THINKING IT THROUGH

Most neighborhoods have a wide variety of available and affordable homes for you. After you have gotten the information needed about the location you like and determined that the house values seem to be in your range, you are ready to take the next step. Find the house you want to buy!

As a single person, buying a home is an emotional and sometimes stressful experience. However, even though you will experience many new emotions, not least of which is fear, try to be realistic about the facts you are facing about the property. A few false starts and a case or two of cold feet are perfectly normal for this kind of major decision.

Take a minute to fill in the following worksheet to help determine the location for your home:

1. Crowded streets with limited parking bother me.   ❏ yes   ❏ no

2. Having neighbors nearby is important to me.   ❏ yes   ❏ no

3. Public transportation must be nearby.   ❏ yes   ❏ no

4. Loud music and parties are okay with me.   ❏ yes   ❏ no

5. Privacy is very important to me.   ❏ yes   ❏ no

6. Do I want restaurants close to my home?   ❏ yes   ❏ no

7. Do I want other singles in my neighborhood?   ❏ yes   ❏ no

8. Do I want an area nearby where I can run or ride my bicycle?   ❏ yes   ❏ no

9. Do I want a gym or health club nearby?   ❏ yes   ❏ no

10. Do I want to have a pet?   ❏ yes   ❏ no

11. Can I walk to work?   ❏ yes   ❏ no

12. Do I want a mall or shopping area nearby?   ❏ yes   ❏ no

13. Do I want night life in the area?

　　　　　　　　　❑ yes　❑ no

If you answered yes to questions 1, 5, and 10, you should definitely consider the rural lifestyle. If you answered yes to questions 2, 3, 6, 12, and 13, the urban lifestyle is probably for you. The future suburbanite will answer yes to questions 2, 8, and 12.

QUICK CHECKLIST
LOCATION

1. Did you check out the schools?

   If you sell later to a family, this may be a key question for them.

2. Did you check out the distance to work?

   If you want to walk or ride your bicycle to work, this may be an important consideration. Long winding roads may become more dangerous in winter.

3. Did you check out the neighborhood at different hours of the day and night?

   Safety when leaving and returning home alone and the safety of friends coming to visit should be important to you. Rush hour traffic can leave you exhausted before you arrive home. Country homes on truck routes can detract from the quiet and privacy of your dream house.

4. Did you check out the school taxes and the property taxes?

   You will need this information for budgeting purposes.

5. Is the area on public water and sewer or well and septic?

   This is especially important if you will have to upgrade to public water and/or sewer from well and septic. It can be quite costly, both in terms of initial costs and future ownership costs reflected in property taxes.

6. Did you check out the condition of the houses next door and across the street?

   You will want to be in a desirable neighborhood that is stable and growing so your investment will grow too.

7. Did you check out the public transportation?

   If you are sensitive to conserving gasoline, this may be important to you.

8. Did you check out the nearest hospital?

   This is always worth noting when searching for your home.

9. Did you check out the distance to shopping areas?

   This is another item for the future sale of your home — convenience for the family shopper.

10. Did you find out what houses in the area had sold for recently?

    It is a good rule of thumb to get acquainted with the area before you buy.

11. Is this neighborhood in your price range?

    If you can find a good deal, you may be able to buy a house valued a bit above what you thought you could afford. Remember that a rundown house in a good neighborhood can be fixed up!

— 4 —
Style and Size

Gary was single again and was used to living in a four-bedroom house with a large lawn in a suburban community. He thought that he would be happier in a much smaller house with less upkeep. He felt like withdrawing from the world for awhile. So Gary decided to buy a small, two-bedroom cottage situated on the back acre of a big farm. The farmer was subdividing some of his land and decided that this old caretaker's house could be sold off first. It was very modest with a small living room, a small kitchen and dining area, a bath with shower stall, and two small bedrooms. Gary felt that this was the perfect cocoon for him at this time. He paid $65,000 for it. He knew that was steep, but he bought it anyway. Just two years later, Gary felt closed in and wanted to move to a larger house again. He finally sold the cottage at a substantial loss. What had Gary forgotten to consider when he bought this out of the way small rural house?

Gary had not realized that size was very important to him. He also forgot that secluded, small, out of the way homes do not appeal to everyone. He would have a more difficult time selling this house in this location when the time came. He thought that other people would see this as a real gem. However, this house will appeal to a smaller market of buyers than a larger house in the suburbs or a townhouse in the city.

STYLES

There are many styles, types, models, shapes, and sizes of houses for singles to choose from in the search for a home. Some are large and some are small. Some have land and some do not. Some stand alone and some are attached. Some are one-story and some are located in a high rise of condominiums. Some are affordable and some are very expensive. The home you choose should combine the features that best suit your needs now.

Common Home Styles

A *split level* home is on multiple levels, often with an integral garage. The levels are divided by steps that separate the living room area from the family room area. Still another set of steps could separate the living room, dining room, and kitchen from the bedrooms and bathroom. Floor plans vary, but multiple levels in the house are characteristic of this house style. A variation of this is the *split foyer*. The main difference in this style home is that steps in the foyer lead up to one part of the house and down to the other. Otherwise, it, too, is a multi-level house.

The *Spanish* style home is distinguished by its tile roof, stucco exterior and interior walls, oval doorways, and central courtyard.

The *ranch* style home is a one-story home low to the ground. These homes vary in size from small homes on a slab with no basement to large "rambling" ranch homes with a full basement and garage. Such a home usually has at least one picture window. The exterior can be brick, stone, siding, cinder block, or combinations of materials. It may have a garage or a carport.

Cape Cod style is a 1 1/2-story house with a shingle roof and central entrance. It may or may not have a basement. The half-story space is usually one or two rooms above the main floor of the house. Some Cape Cod homes are small, while others are very spacious.

Dutch Colonial style is 2 1/2 stories with a gambrel roof, dormers, and a front Dutch door. The half floor is above the second floor of bedrooms. These are generally large, four- to six-bedroom homes. Such a home usually has a full basement and a two-car garage.

A *French Provincial* home is 1 1/2 to 2 1/2 stories with curved window trim that extends through the cornice. It has a steep hip roof design of slate or shingle. A full basement is common.

The *Georgian* style home has chimneys at either end and a hip roof, and is usually brick. A full basement is common. These are also large homes with at least three bedrooms.

Colonial style is two to three stories, symmetrical, with a column-supported colonnade. The home can be faced in brick, stucco, stone, or siding. It usually has a full basement, and it is common to see shutters at each window. This style home also often has a garage.

Row houses are especially common in cities and are often referred to by city block. For example, "the 1400 block of Maple Street." Each house is attached and separated by a fire wall. They are usually two-story, but can be found in one-story and three-story also. A row house may or may not have a basement or garage. The house can be faced in brick, stone, or siding with a slate, tile, or shingle roof. They are usually three-bedroom homes and are very popular in the city.

Townhouse style is a cluster of one- or two-story houses sharing a common wall. A townhouse may be on a slab or have a basement, and it may or may not have a garage. Frequently, the common grounds and exterior upkeep are maintained by a home-owners' association. The owner pays a monthly fee for these services. Some developments have a swimming pool and tennis courts for the residents to use as part of the association fees or other form of membership.

A *condominium* is simply an individually owned unit (like an apartment) in a larger building or group of buildings. It commonly has a living room, dining area, kitchen, one or two bathrooms, two to four bedrooms, and sometimes a balcony or porch. This type of housing also has a condominium association and maintenance and service fees for the common grounds.

Uncommon Styles

Be on the lookout for the home that does not seem to fit the prevailing style of the neighborhood. If all the homes in a particular area are ranch-style, except the one you are considering, which is a Spanish-style adobe villa, beware. It will be much harder to sell a home that does not look like its neighbors should you decide to do so down the road. It is also true that it will be much harder to sell a home that is either much larger or much smaller than its neighbors — a two-bedroom cottage in a subdivision of four-bedroom Colonials, for example.

There are as many variations and combinations of the various home styles as there are potential buyers. Look at as many different styles as possible to determine what you like best. If you decide you hate split-foyer homes, don't look at any more. But even if you decide Cape Cod is the style for you, don't necessarily rule out all other styles. You may find the floor plan or special interior features of the home is even more important than its general exterior appearance.

FLOOR PLANS

The home's floor plan is very important to your comfort and convenience, as well as to future resale value. A home with a conventional floor plan is much more efficient than a home with, for in-

STYLE AND SIZE   25

stance, a floor plan requiring access to one bedroom through another. Don't necessarily rule out such a home, but consider it carefully before making the decision to purchase. The minimum you should expect from a conventional floor plan is a living room, dining area (or eat-in kitchen) adjacent to the kitchen, and bedroom(s) and bathroom(s) accessed from a main hallway.

SIZE

The size of the home you choose is very important for a number of reasons. You want a home that is large enough to be comfortable but not so large that maintenance is overwhelming. If you plan to subsidize your costs with a housemate who pays rent, you will need enough space so you are not tripping over each other. As mentioned above, certain styles of homes have the size (specifically, number of bedrooms) almost built in. You may not want to set your heart on a Dutch Colonial — those six bedrooms may cost you a lot more than you can afford. In general, the larger the home, the more it will cost. This is so basic, it almost goes without saying, but there are some pitfalls to be aware of. A home could be advertised as "four bedrooms," but one of those bedrooms (maybe even two!) could be in the basement. This factor could bring the price down into your range; could you use some extra space for an exercise room or a home office?

A home that is too small may leave you feeling cramped and claustrophobic. If you already have a great deal of furniture — maybe you collect and refinish antiques as a hobby — will it all fit in a small home? In addition, a very important factor is that homes with only two bedrooms are simply not

as easy to sell as homes with three or four bedrooms. Even though you are a single person — you don't think you will ever need three bedrooms — don't rule out three-bedroom homes in your search. Unless you plan to live in this house forever, you will have much better luck selling a home with more than two bedrooms.

QUICK CHECKLIST
STYLE AND SIZE

1. Are the size and style compatible with the neighborhood, or is the house so unusual that it is a "white elephant"?

2. Does the home have at least three bedrooms?

3. Is the size of the yard, if it has one, manageable for you or will you need more than a small lawn mower?

4. Is the exterior of the house considered to be low maintenance or will it need to be painted regularly?

5. Is there a maintenance or condominium association fee?

6. Are the houses in the neighborhood in good repair (allowing for good resale prices)?

7. Is the house the size you wanted?

8. Is the house a size and style that is popular and easy to resell?

9. Are you being realistic about size and price?

10. Are you satisfied with the location for this style and size home?

11. Is the price inflated or fair? Check others in the neighborhood.

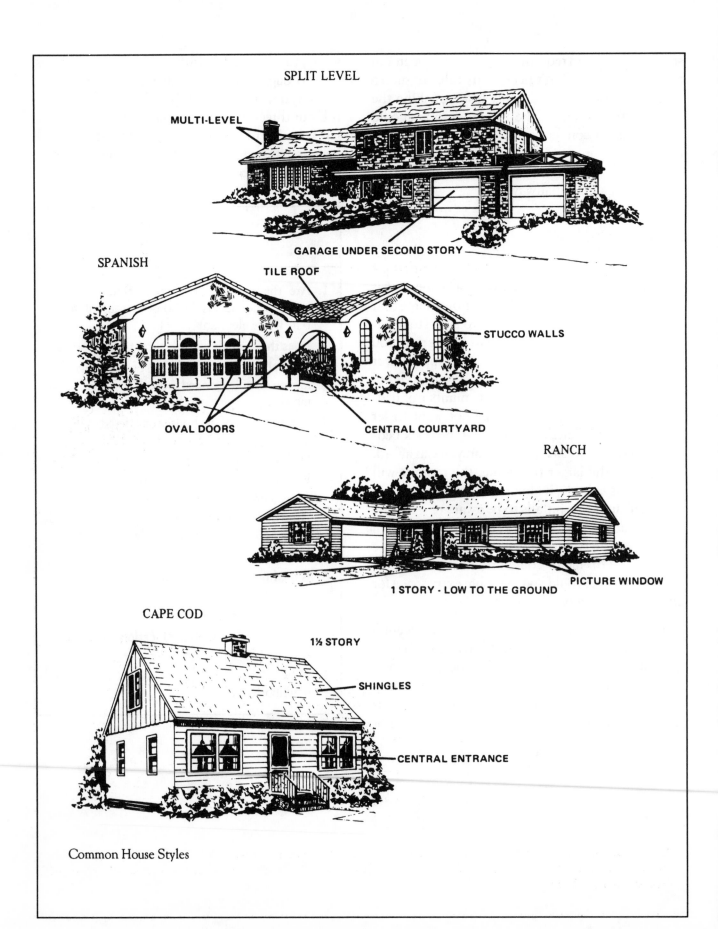

Common House Styles

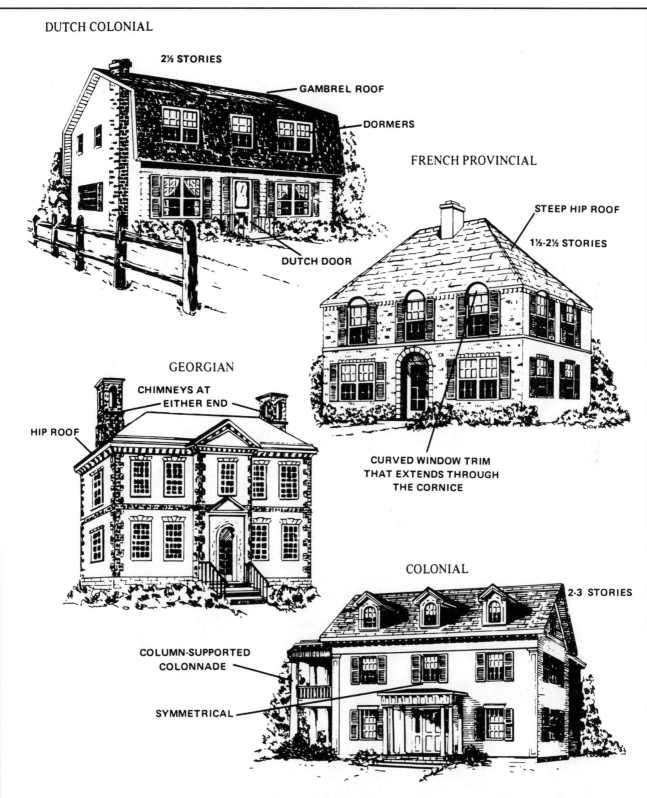

DUTCH COLONIAL

2½ STORIES

GAMBREL ROOF

DORMERS

DUTCH DOOR

FRENCH PROVINCIAL

STEEP HIP ROOF

1½-2½ STORIES

CURVED WINDOW TRIM
THAT EXTENDS THROUGH
THE CORNICE

GEORGIAN

CHIMNEYS AT
EITHER END

HIP ROOF

COLONIAL

2-3 STORIES

COLUMN-SUPPORTED
COLONNADE

SYMMETRICAL

Used with permission: *Modern Real Estate Practice in Pennsylvania*, 5th edition, Bellairs, Helsel, Caldwell. Copyright © 1989 by Dearborn Financial Publishing, Inc. Published by Real Estate Education Company, a Division of Dearborn Financial Publishing Inc., Chicago.

— 5 —
When to Buy

Julie taught school and had planned to begin her house search in May, hoping to find what she wanted, at the price she could afford. She hoped to settle before the school year began in late August. She knew that there were often more houses available in the spring. She also knew that prices tended to be a bit higher. She had been thinking about this move for a very long time and had decided to proceed, even if all conditions in the market were not ideal for home buyers. Do you think that Julie is wise to go ahead with her plan?

Julie has been planning her move and is making a good decision. She could wait a very long time for conditions to be "ideal." Remember: Dreamers may never move while movers may find their dream!

The question of timing is often asked. There are answers to suit every buyer and every seller. But is there, in fact, a time of the year — spring, winter, or other — that may make a difference? Consider several factors when asking yourself this question.

SCHOOL YEAR OR FALL AND SPRING

The typical school year is September to June, and this fact influences a number of sales cycles in our economy. As for buying a home, if you are a single parent with children of school age, it could influence you to schedule your move in the summer months when school is not in session. You would try to have your closing, or settlement, scheduled anytime from June to August. That would encourage a seller to list his or her house for sale in early spring. This may be the most convenient time for you to buy, but prices may not be in your favor.

Prices are typically highest from early spring to early to midsummer. A seller putting his house on the market at this time may be setting as high a price as he figures the market will bear. He may be counting on the house selling anytime within six to nine months, so he is willing to wait. He may also be just "testing the water"; he is putting his house on the market, asking an inflated price for it, just to see if he can sell it. This is another instance when it is important to check comparables before making an offer.

WINTER

Winter is often a good time for buyers to find the right house at the right price. Prices are often lower in late fall and winter, because sellers may be desperate or simply philosophical about asking a lower price, knowing that traditionally housing prices are down at this time of year.

Many sellers worry about selling their homes in the winter because of uncertain weather conditions, and often set the price for quick sale. This is especially true if the property owner has been trying with little luck to sell the house, or the house is vacant and not well winterized.

December ends a tax year, and for some buyers that may be the best time to buy. Keep in mind, however, that if you buy late in the year, you will not have the tax benefits of writing off large amounts of interest on your mortgage loan. (You will still be able to deduct points and some closing costs.) January begins a new tax year and for some buyers that might be the best time to buy.

Your accountant and your Realtor should be able to help you on these issues of timing and taxes.

SUMMER

Summer is traditionally a popular time to settle on a property and to plan a move during vacation time. The weather is usually cooperative as well. Just remember, in order to move into your new home during the summer, you will have to begin your work at least three to six months ahead of your goal date.

Whatever season of the year you decide to buy your home, you will want to ask some questions. You will want to find out everything that you can about this house and the neighborhood you have chosen. Talk to the neighbors. Visit nearby schools, stores, parks. Get acquainted with the area. Make a checklist of questions for yourself.

MORTGAGE RATES

Mortgage rates are always a consideration when buying a home. When the economy is strong and growing, it is not uncommon for mortgage rates to be rather high and even double digit if inflation gets out of control. When the economy is weaker or flat with slow growth, it is likely that the mortgage rates will fall to lower levels. When the rates are lower, buyers are encouraged to buy if they can. Lower interest rates make buying a home more affordable for everyone.

In addition, lower interest rates may encourage homeowners to "move up" to a higher-priced home by putting their homes on the market. Lower interest rates are usually reflected in an increase in the number of homes coming on the market.

Property prices or the fair market value of homes will vary with the economic indicators as well. Sometimes we refer to a buyer's *market* or a *seller's market*. It is not difficult to know which type of market you are currently experiencing as you start home shopping. If interest rates are under 10% and property values are fair, you will be able to afford to buy. If interest rates are above 10% and property values are inflated, buying a home will be more difficult. Keep in mind that lenders are becoming more and more stringent in their standards to qualify a buyer.

TAXES

Every year we go through a cycle of taxes. When you become a homeowner, you will be faced with real estate taxes, school taxes, and city taxes. It is important to understand this so that you can budget properly. Consider too that if you expect an income tax refund, it may help you toward a springtime home purchase.

At any rate, taxes will be a factor to consider when buying a home. Consider that many of the costs of buying the home can be taken as tax deductions. Be careful to check this with your accountant so that you understand how the purchase will affect you at tax time.

As a single person, you may need some tax shelter. Home ownership may be a good idea for you.

QUICK CHECKLIST WHEN TO BUY

1. Have you determined the most convenient time for you to make a move?
2. Have you planned to start looking for a home three to six months ahead of your ideal moving date?
3. Do you check the local lenders' residential mortgage rates on a regular basis?
4. Do you keep an eye on home prices in the area you are interested in?
5. Will your employer move you if the house you choose is somewhere else or is there a possibility of being transferred?
6. Will the school year influence the time you will buy?

— 6 —
Working with a Realtor

Ellen, like many naive first-time single buyers, called a local real estate agency one Saturday to inquire about a house she had seen with the agency's sale sign on it. The agent who answered the telephone was "on duty" at that time and became Ellen's agent. He set up an appointment for Ellen to see the house she had called about in addition to several other properties. Ellen noticed that the agent showed properties that did not fit her description or desired location. Most of the properties he showed were his own listings. After months of frustration, Ellen gave up her search altogether. How could Ellen have found a more compatible real estate agent?

There are several things Ellen could have done to find a compatible agent. She could have asked an associate or a friend for a referral to someone they had worked with and liked. She could have asked specifically for the agent named on the sale sign instead of working with the agent on duty. She could check that the Realtor is a member of the National Association of Realtors, which indicates that he or she operates by the Code of Ethics and Standards. She could consider, if such a service is available, entering into a contract with a Realtor for a flat fee to work only for her, the buyer.

HOW TO FIND A REALTOR

How do you find a Realtor who suits you? This is a very good question. Some people are very happy working with anyone from a well-established real estate firm in the area. Still other people will search long and hard for a compatible agent.

Referral is one of the best ways to find a Realtor. Ask friends, coworkers, and people whose judgment you trust for referrals to good Realtors. Then ask why they like the particular Realtor. If the answer is that the Realtor gave them great advice, helped find the perfect home, and assisted throughout the contract and settlement process, give that Realtor a call. But if you find you don't click with your friend's Realtor, keep looking. There is nothing worse than making a commitment to a Realtor only to find you are very uncomfortable answering the kinds of personal questions the Realtor will have to ask.

Another benefit of asking for referrals is that you may get some names of Realtors to avoid. If your coworker talks about a Realtor who lied to her or failed to assist adequately, run in the opposite direction.

If you can't find a Realtor by word of mouth, there are other options. Look at "For Sale" signs for names that appear regularly. Then interview those Realtors and ask for referrals to past buyers.

Remember, just because you have spoken to one Realtor does not mean you have made a firm commitment to that person. It is certainly to your advantage to work with only one Realtor at a time;

if the Realtor knows you are working with several people, he may not do his best in the face of such competition. But if you feel uncomfortable, pressured, or not listened to, feel free to drop that Realtor and look elsewhere.

Be aware that there is a Code of Ethics and Standards of Practice for Realtors who are members of The National Association of Realtors. In fact, be sure that you are working with a Realtor member. For example, in the Preamble of the National Association of Realtors Code of Ethics it states:

> *The term Realtor has come to connote competency, fairness, and high integrity resulting from adherence to a lofty ideal of moral conduct in business relations. No inducement of profit and no instruction from clients ever can justify departure from this ideal.*

TYPES OF REALTORS

If you choose to work with a Realtor, then you need to decide who to work with to locate your home. Remember that the Realtor is the agent for the seller. A Realtor earns a commission on the sale of the house. Be sure to understand that it is not necessarily your best interest that is being served. You as the buyer must be aware and knowledgeable. This is your responsibility! On the other hand, working with a Realtor can be a real timesaver. The Realtor handles the details to bring the sale to a smooth settlement.

Seller's Broker
The seller's broker is the Realtor to whom the seller has entrusted the sale of her home. The seller enters into a contract with the seller's broker for the sale of the home. This creates a business relationship in which the Realtor is working, usually exclusively, for the seller.

Let's say you have not previously been working with a Realtor, and you find the home you want. You contact the Realtor whose name is on the "For Sale" sign (he is probably the same person who showed you the home) and approach him about a contract. This situation may work out just fine for you, if you are aware of the potential pitfalls. The goal of the seller's broker is to sell the property quickly for the highest price. His loyalty is to the seller, with whom he has a contract. He has no loyalty to you as the buyer. It is not his job to help you determine the amount of your offer; in fact, he cannot do this by virtue of his contract with the seller and the Code of Ethics mentioned above. If you are prepared to do a lot of the legwork yourself — researching comparables, determining a price to offer — go ahead. But there are potentially better alternatives.

Buyer's Realtor
The buyer's Realtor, or buyer's agent, is the traditional way to go. In this instance, you have an informal (i.e., not on paper) agreement for the Realtor to help you find the home you want. She will pre-qualify you to determine how much you can afford, help you find potential properties, arrange for viewing homes, and pretty much hold your hand throughout the search process. However, when the time comes to offer a contract, the situation changes. Her allegiance will switch from you to the seller. The buyer's Realtor will help you prepare an offer to purchase, but she will not help you determine a purchase price. It is her job at this time to obtain the best possible purchase price *for the seller*. Again, if you do your homework and feel quite confident about making an offer to purchase, that is great and you should go ahead.

Using a buyer's Realtor is certainly the most common working arrangement for a buyer and a Realtor. However, an alternative has recently entered the scene, which offers great possibilities.

Buyer's Broker
The concept of the buyer's broker is rapidly gaining acceptance. In this arrangement, the buyer and the Realtor enter into a contract in which the Realtor agrees to work only for the buyer. The Realtor is often paid solely by the buyer on a flat fee or percentage basis rather than out of the commission

from the purchase of the home. The buyer's broker should be prepared to offer current market data, prepare lists of comparables, assist in getting financing, and, most important, help write the purchase offer that is most favorable to you. While the buyer's broker may not directly answer the question, "What do you think I should offer?" However, the scenario could go something like this.

Buyer: "Given the asking price of $103,000, do you think an offer of $96,500 is insultingly low?"

Buyer's Broker: "No. While the seller is probably not going to accept an offer that low, it is a good starting place for further negotiation."

Buyer: "And we have set my upper limit as $101,000?"

Buyer's Broker: "Right. But we might want to consider asking the seller to pay some closing costs. If you are not comfortable at your upper limit, that could take some of the pressure off and give us another bargaining chip as well."

Buyer: "Okay. Let's offer $96,500 and see what happens. I hope we can get it for around $100,000."

Call local real estate firms and ask which Realtors will work in a buyer's broker relationship. It is well worth your investigation, especially if this is the first home you have bought, to have someone exclusively on your team.

WORKING WITH A REALTOR

Once you have found the Realtor you want to work with, it is time to share your preferred location and the house size and style you want with your Realtor. Be realistic about the price range you can afford. Your Realtor should ask a number of questions about your financial status and how you plan to finance the home you want to buy. This information will help establish whether you are a "qualified" buyer for the type of home that you have described. The Realtor may even take you to a mortgage lender and pre-qualify you with him or her. This is a great idea and may give you some

insights into the closing costs you should expect. Pre-qualifying with a mortgage lender in no way obligates you to use that lender when you apply for your loan.

It is important to be absolutely honest with your Realtor regarding your financial status. When you go to apply for your mortgage loan, the lender will find out everything anyway, including your credit history, employment and salary, and credit card balances. The Realtor can only be helpful to you if you are completely up-front with her. It would be disastrous to find yourself in love with a house $20,000 out of your price range because you had fudged a few figures.

The Realtor will show you a number of listings, probably from her Multiple Listing Service book. Some will be listings the Realtor has from her sellers. Others will be listings of other Realtors in the firm. And still others will be listings from other firms. You will be given an opportunity to look at the homes you choose. The Realtor will arrange with the seller to show you the property.

You will be shown some properties that do not resemble your "dream house" in the least. Be sure to keep the Realtor on track for you. It is always a temptation for the Realtor to show you what she has listed, regardless of the size and type of house that you have described. Often she will tell you that she can get the house at a good price and that you really should consider it. That is up to you. You may decide to look at a wide variety of houses. My suggestion would be to limit your search to fit into the location, size and type, price range, and structural condition of the house you had in mind to begin this search. Try not to become overwhelmed with choices. Be sure to express your feelings to your Realtor and be specific: "I loved the hardwood floors, but the kitchen is just too small." "I'm afraid I couldn't keep up with a yard this size." "The master bath is just what I wanted." If you cannot be specific about your likes and dislikes with your Realtor, she will not be able to narrow down the choices for you. Be honest; it can only work to your advantage.

The Realtor plays a vital role in bringing the buyer and seller to an agreement, if possible. The Realtor will relay your questions to the seller and the answers to you. If you find a house that you especially like, do not hesitate to go back to see it more than once before you decide to make an offer. The Realtor will be glad to accommodate you on this request. Bring a friend as a sounding board and for moral support. It would be helpful if your friend owned a house and had some experience to share with you.

QUICK CHECKLIST
WORKING WITH A REALTOR

1. Have you asked a friend or coworker about a Realtor he or she would recommend?

2. Have you talked to people in the area about the local real estate agencies? Do they have good reputations?

3. Do you understand that the Realtor is the agent for the seller?

4. Have you explored the possibility of using a buyer's broker?

5. Do you know that you need not continue working with a Realtor who does not provide you with the level of service you expect?

6. Once you have found a Realtor you trust, do you understand why it is important to be absolutely honest regarding your financial status?

7. Do you understand the role of the Realtor in bringing the buyer and seller together in an agreement if possible?

— 7 —

Selecting a Lawyer

John is a single parent who wanted to move from an apartment to a house in a good school district near his work. He knew the area he liked and was hoping to be settled into a new house by the end of August. He had a friend in law school whom he called on to help him. The two of them learned together about the agreement of sale and what procedures were standard in such a transaction. John felt unsure. So did his friend. What could John have done to have made a better decision in selecting a lawyer?

John could have sought an experienced lawyer. If cost was a factor, he needs to realize that he is ensuring a smooth settlement and perhaps avoiding costly errors when the final agreement is signed. John must understand the importance of a competent lawyer who is experienced in real estate transactions. His lawyer will look to protect him in this legal transaction. Usually a seller will have legal counsel at settlement. The buyer should be represented too.

It is important for you to know that lawyers, like physicians, practice specialties. Not every lawyer is either well trained or even interested in real estate contracts. Your first step is to check carefully into the legal services you choose.

Be certain that the lawyer you are going to work with is very knowledgeable in real estate law and contracts so that your experience in these negotiations to buy a house is handled well. Ask your lawyer if this is of interest to him. Your lawyer will work on your behalf. If you are not working with a Realtor, your lawyer can present your offer to the seller. Otherwise, this will be done by the Realtor. It is completely up to you whether or not you use the services of a lawyer or Realtor or choose to use both.

BEGINNING THE SEARCH

You can begin your search for a qualified lawyer in several ways. The following list will help you begin this process. Add other ways as you think of them.

1. Ask your friends if they would recommend their lawyer for this task.

2. Ask your employer for suggestions on whom to use for this important transaction.

3. Search for lawyers or law firms in the telephone book yellow pages. Many times, they will list their specialties.

4. Ask your banker, if the bank is local, if he would suggest a lawyer for this job. If you plan to get your mortgage loan from this bank, the bank will usually have a lawyer overseeing your application at settlement. However, the in-house lawyer may not be available to you.

5. Telephone the local bar association's lawyer referral service for a list of lawyers who specialize in residential real estate transactions.

WHAT YOUR LAWYER CAN DO FOR YOU

When you identify the lawyer you wish to work with on this transaction, be sure to establish beforehand the fee for this service. Also have the lawyer work up an estimate of settlement costs so that you are well aware of the figures. If you are working with a Realtor, she will provide you with the Buyer's Costs Estimate Sheet as part of the services provided. Frequently, your lawyer will be willing to give you advice on the deal you propose. Usually, he is well aware of potential legal issues and will work with you and for your protection.

What if the seller changes his mind about selling after the agreement of sale is signed? Call your lawyer. What if the seller comes to settlement without completing the terms of the agreement? Have your lawyer at settlement. What if the seller accepts rent from a tenant in the house for a month beyond the settlement date? Call your lawyer. What if vandals damage the vacant property before settlement? Call your lawyer. Needless to say, having a lawyer working to protect you is one of the best things you can do for yourself.

It is important, however, that you and your lawyer can communicate. Ask yourself if your lawyer explains things to you or "snows" you, talks too fast, seems preoccupied, and does not return your telephone calls, or responds quickly to your concerns and is efficient in handling your questions.

Once you have found a house for sale and like it and want to buy it, your next step is to make the offer. If you do not have a Realtor to work with on this sale, then your lawyer can act on your behalf and convey your offer to the seller. In any event, it is a wise idea to have your lawyer review the contract for its legal soundness.

If your lawyer is going to represent you to the seller, you will give the lawyer your earnest money deposit. Your lawyer will prepare the paperwork necessary for the offer. Once both the seller and the buyer agree and sign the agreement for the sale, the agreement is a legally binding contract.

Whether I am working with a Realtor or not, I always have my lawyer with me at settlement when I buy property. It is sometimes necessary to work out last-minute unexpected issues at settlement. For example, going over the buyer's cost sheet can be a bit confusing, and having your lawyer with you will add to your confidence in the proceedings.

QUICK CHECKLIST SELECTING A LAWYER

1. Do you know a lawyer who specializes in real estate contracts?
2. Have you asked a friend or an employer for a reference to a lawyer?
3. Is there a local bar association lawyer referral service available?
4. Did you check in the local telephone directory?
5. Do you know a lawyer who would refer you to a firm in the area where you plan to move?
6. Have you established the fee for legal services?
7. Will your lawyer come with you to settlement?
8. Do you trust your lawyer's judgment?
9. Would you recommend your lawyer or law firm to a friend?
10. Does your lender or Realtor know of your lawyer because of his reputation in real estate matters?

— 8 —
How to Find a Seller

Lisa was determined to buy her first house without the help of a Realtor. She wanted to prove to herself that she could find the house she wanted on her own. So Lisa began to drive around the area every Saturday morning looking for houses with homemade "For Sale" signs. Lisa searched and searched. She began to look in the newspaper for advertisements of homes for sale by owner. Lisa called many of these owners, but found that they were asking very high prices for their homes. She even went to see a few houses. She felt frustrated with her search. She also began to believe that people were not being very honest with her about the condition of their homes. Lisa had no experience with home owner-ship and wasn't sure what to ask. She hoped the seller would volunteer all the information. What could Lisa have done to make this search more successful?

Lisa must write up a list of specific questions about the property that she wants answered. She should gather information about the history of the house: how many owners, has it been rented, is there evidence of termites, and so on. She could ask for a data sheet on the house so that she can see taxes, utility expenses, and lot size. When Lisa looks at the house, she will have to be aware of what to look for in electrical service, plumbing, and structural soundness. She will want to have the house inspected by a professional. (This is true whether she uses a Realtor or not.) She may decide to work with a Realtor.

WORKING WITHOUT A REALTOR

When you decide to work on your own to find a house, you will need to plan all the moves a Realtor would be doing for you. You will need to determine how much house you can afford; arrange to look at properties; find the house you think you want; check on the history of the property; work directly with the seller on structural or cosmetic issues; negotiate the price; and be aware of legal issues. You must be thorough.

How do you find a seller if you decide not to work with a Realtor? The following list will give you some ideas. Add to the list if you can.

Ways to Find a Seller

1. Check the newspaper for estate sales and con-tact the executor or executrix. An address or a telephone number is usually listed. If not, a lawyer's name will be listed. Contact the law-yer.

2. Read the newspaper and courthouse lists for delinquent tax sales in the area. Prepare to go to the sale with your offer. Check in the courthouse for the details, procedures, dates, and times for the public sale.

3. Observe very carefully if a house in the area seems to be abandoned or vacant for a long

period of time. Go to the courthouse to find out who the owner is. Write to him or her with your interest in buying the property.

4. Talk to friends and acquaintances about your interest in buying a house in their neighborhood and tell them to call you if they hear of something.

5. Make up a flyer and put it in the doors of homes you would be interested in buying. Be sure to leave a telephone number or address where you can be reached.

6. Place an ad in the local newspaper describing basically the style of home you are looking to buy and when you would need to be in the house. Be aware that this approach will also bring Realtors to you, with or without the house that you describe.

7. Look for homemade "For Sale" signs. The owner is obviously trying to sell the house without a Realtor.

8. Find out if a property in the area is presently being rented. Usually the neighbors will know. Contact the owner to see if he would be interested in selling the property to you.

9. Sometimes you will see new developments or subdivisions in a growing area. Often, you can buy directly from the developer. Check it out.

10. Talk with your bank mortgage loan officer for information on loans in jeopardy. (This information may or may not be available to you.)

11. Ask the people in the neighborhood you have chosen if they know of anyone who might be retiring and would like to sell their home.

THE SEARCH

You may be able to add to this list. These ideas will help you find a house in the area that you have selected for your home. This search will take time, patience, and skill. In a sense, you are doing the footwork of a Realtor. It is not easy work. Does your work schedule allow time for all this footwork?

Doing your homework in every aspect of home buying is critical. I am sure that you have heard the saying "buyer beware"! Being an informed buyer is the best way to assure yourself of a good, sound, solid start as a single homeowner.

QUICK CHECKLIST
FINDING A SELLER

1. Have you driven around the areas you like, looking for "For Sale" signs?

2. Have you decided to work with a Realtor?

3. Have you been watching the classified section of homes for sale?

4. Have you told your friends that you are looking for a house?

5. Have you decided to make up a flyer to distribute in the neighborhood, telling of your interest in buying a home there?

6. Have you decided to place an ad describing the home and price range you are looking for in the area?

7. Have you talked with your local banker about houses that may be available?

8. Have you talked to any of the neighbors?

9. Have you done your homework — determining price range of homes in the area you like?

10. Do you know what questions to ask? Are there any deed restrictions? What is the zoning of the house you want to buy? Remember, if you have a pet, and the deed restricts building a fence, you need to know *before* you buy the house that you cannot fence the yard.

— 9 —
The Agreement of Sale

Charles was middle-aged when he decided to buy his first house. He found what he wanted and made his offer through a Realtor. He had carefully thought through the price he would offer, the date he proposed to settle, the percentage of sales tax each would pay. He felt pleased with his offer. He settled on his house on schedule. Only after settlement did he question the two malfunctioning window air conditioners and the lack of storm windows; items he had assumed were in good working order and complete, but had not specified in writing under the fixtures clause in the agreement. What should Charles have done to avoid these surprises?

Charles would not have had this surprise had he had all of his expectations for these items negotiated ahead of time and clearly stated in the Agreement of Sale. Charles is not alone in this error. We all assume things at times. This is not the time to assume anything! Be sure to put conditions of the sale in writing in the contingency section of the Agreement of Sale.

AGREEMENT OF SALE

You must have an Agreement of Sale, or contract, signed by the buyer and seller before you can begin processing your mortgage request. The Realtor or your lawyer can put this together for you.

Look over the Sample Agreement of Sale carefully. Work out the costs so that you are well informed on this part of the transaction. Make a list of questions for your lawyer or Realtor to answer.

Although it may seem complicated at first glance, each part of the Agreement of Sale plays an important role in the transaction. It is a contract and is legally binding.

Putting together an Agreement of Sale is a tricky part of the process of buying a house. If you are working with a Realtor, especially if the property you want to buy is the Realtor's own listing, it may go more easily because the Realtor has a good idea what the seller will settle for in the transaction. The Realtor will guide you and the seller toward the agreement needed to have a sale. The Realtor often knows what price the seller will ultimately take for the house. The Realtor also has a good idea of what conditions of sale will make or break the deal.

1. PRINCIPALS: The seller will be named first, and then you, the buyer, will be named second. Use the exact name you will want on all transactions for this house.

2. PROPERTY: Use the exact address of the property you want to buy. (Your Realtor or lawyer can look up the lot and block number used as a legal description of the property's location.)

3. ZONING: Generally, your house will be in a residential zone. Commercial, industrial, and mixed zones can also be found. Each area has its own set of restrictions. Check it out.

4. TERMS: The terms clearly state the following.

a. The purchase price you have agreed to pay.

b. The amount of the deposit you have put up front with the offer.

c. Any additional money needed and when you will pay it.

d. The balance due, which is usually the amount you will borrow in the mortgage and will pay at settlement.

e. The date specified asks that the seller respond to the buyer in order to close the deal or counter the offer with other terms.

f. This date is set for settlement on the sale. Usually thirty to sixty days from the acceptance of the offer to the closing is proposed.

g. This item varies in different states, but usually taxes and assorted fees are pro-rated and shared by the buyer and the seller on the day of settlement.

5. PROPERTY SETTLEMENT: Unless you own a house that you must sell before the lender will approve your loan, this item will not apply to you. Chances are, this is your first house as a single person, so this item will be left blank or N/A.

6. FINANCING CONTINGENCY: If you are able to pay in cash, this item will be blank. Otherwise, the information needed here is amount of the mortgage loan ($50,000), the type of loan you will apply for (Conventional), for the term (30 years), at the current interest rate (8%). The TERMINAL DATE to get financing is important because if you fail to get a mortgage loan commitment by the date set (usually four to six weeks), the agreement is null and void with no penalties as long as you have been rejected in your attempts to find financing. In this case, you will receive your down payment back in full, and the contract is null and void between you and the seller. Read the small print here to become familiar with the contingencies.

7. INFORMATION ITEM: The status of WATER and SEWER is designed to identify properties with water service or well water and sewer systems or septic tanks. Safety inspec-tions are usually needed to assess the water quality and the septic system condition.

8. MUNICIPAL IMPROVEMENTS: This usually refers to sewer or water lines. If the property you plan to buy is already on public water and sewer, you will not have to worry. If not, you may have to pay your share of the improvements when they are done.

9. SPECIAL CLAUSES: You can write in here whatever you and the seller have agreed to include in or exclude from the sale. It may be air conditioners, washer and dryer, refrigerator, items of furnishings, and so forth. These are the negotiable items between the buyer and seller.

10. ATTACHED ADDENDA: Depending on your part of the country, these attachments can include infestation report, radon disclosure, private water/septic quality status, and others.

11. PERSONALTY: Here you can state the items that remain, such as fireplace grate and glass door, stove, all fixtures attached to the ceilings and walls, outdoor shed, storm windows, and other items considered to be part of the house.

12-23. INFORMATION: These items regard other legal actions related to the transfer of property ownership. Read each statement so that you are familiar with the agreement you will be signing.

When you make an offer, be sure that you are being fair and reasonable. The owner often believes the property is worth considerably more than can be gotten in the market. Unless the asking price is agreeable to you and you offer that price, you will have to make an offer that is within the ballpark of fair market value. If you have done your homework — checking comparable properties, having the house inspected — you should have a very good idea of the value of the property. If the property needs some work, an owner might be willing to take a lower price based on taking the property "as is" rather than requiring that repairs be done before settlement.

CONTINGENCIES

There are a number of contingencies you may want to add to the Agreement of Sale. Discuss these with your Realtor — he or she will be able to advise you regarding which contingencies you will need.

Financing Contingency

The financing contingency is included in almost all purchase offers. It spells out the financing terms and the type of financing you want, as well as a time frame for getting financing. If you include a financing contingency, be sure it states that if you are unable to obtain financing, the contract is null and void.

Inspection Contingency

The inspection contingency is optional but highly recommended. It gives you the opportunity to have the property professionally inspected for defects within a certain time frame (usually just a couple of days). Normally, after the inspection is completed, if there are any problems that the seller needs to address, he or she is given the option (in writing, of course) to do so. If the seller prefers not to do the necessary repairs, the contract may have to be re-negotiated. (If the seller refuses to accept a contract with an inspection contingency, take the hint. Run, don't walk, in the other direction.)

Title Search and Survey Contingencies

In many cases, the title search and survey contingencies are required by the mortgage lender. These are fairly standard contingencies and usually won't affect acceptance of the contract. The title search is designed to ensure that you get "good and marketable" title to the property. The survey will determine exactly the perimeters of the property, any structures on the property, and whether there are any zoning restrictions or easements in effect.

NEGOTIATION

It is highly likely that you will find yourself in a negotiation. It is not uncommon to make an offer and to receive a counter-offer to which you make another counter-offer and so on until an agreement is reached.

Know what you can afford! Know your uppermost possible offer and go no higher. Also know what the property is worth. You should make your initial offer based on what you think the property is worth, what you know you can afford, and what the seller is likely to accept. Of course, the seller wants an offer for his full price (preferably in cash and closing tomorrow!), but you almost certainly don't want to make your initial offer for the full price. Your best bet is to make the lowest offer you think the owner will not find insulting. You should not offer $60,000 for a house with an asking price of $100,000, when the comparables indicate that its value is in the $90,000 to $95,000 range.

Let's say you are looking at this $100,000 house. The upper limit of your comfort zone is $97,000. You have done your research and determined the home's assessed value — $92,500. Comparable homes are running $94,000 to $98,500. Your initial offer might be $93,000. The seller counters with $98,000 and offers to pay $1,000 of your closing costs. Now you know that the seller is basically prepared to come down at least $1,000 — he is going to spend that money out of pocket, isn't he? You counter again with $95,000 but you take out the line about his paying closing costs. The seller accepts your offer and everyone is happy.

Don't be surprised if your negotiations go back and forth in this manner. Yes, it is nerve-racking, but the process takes a lot less time than you might think, and it is well worth your time and effort to try to get your best price.

There are many reasons people sell houses. If you can, it is always good to find out the reason for the sale of the property you are considering. The following list reflects some of the possible reasons:

- moving to another location to work or retire
- divorce that forces a sale to settle the issues
- death of a spouse
- death or long-term illness that leaves a property vacant

- moving to a smaller house or a larger house
- threatened foreclosure or back taxes that forces a sale

Depending on the reason, the sale price will be more or less negotiable. It is up to you to negotiate to the best of your ability in this matter. Don't be afraid to stand your ground. Even if you love everything about the house you have chosen, it is not worth it to go above your price limit and end up in foreclosure proceedings a year later. If your Realtor is acting as buyer's broker, she should be very helpful in the negotiation process. She will help you determine your original offer (not too high, not too low) and will understand the finer points of negotiating a real estate contract.

PRESENTING THE OFFER

Either the Realtor or your lawyer, if you are not working with a Realtor, will present your offer to the seller. A time for a response is usually established in the presentation, item 4(e) on the sample Agreement of Sale. The seller can accept, reject, or counter your offer. Unless your offer is very far from a fair market value, the seller will probably counter your offer with some of your conditions accepted and some not accepted.

When an agreement is reached, both parties sign the Agreement of Sale. Each of the parties gets a copy of the signed Agreement of Sale. You are now ready to carry out the conditions of the sale, as is the seller. You have a legally binding contract in the Agreement of Sale, and you can proceed to the lending institution to apply for your mortgage loan.

BUYER'S REMORSE

Buyer's remorse is a phenomenon almost everyone experiences, particularly when buying a first home. It is the feeling you get after you have signed all the contracts, the seller has accepted your offer, and you have filled out the numerous forms to apply for your mortgage loan. Then it hits. "What am I doing? I didn't really like that house nearly as much as the one on Elm Street that was $12,000 more. Of course, the Elm Street house was out of my price range and under contract, but still ... I must be out of my mind. What am I getting myself into? What if I close on this house and then decide I hate it?"

If it is any comfort, as I said, almost everyone experiences these feelings. For the single buyer, the feelings may be even stronger than for the traditional couple, who at least have someone else to blame! If you have a good Realtor, he will be aware of your feelings and be prepared to help you through this difficult period. You may want to talk it through with him. He will remind you of all the things you loved about the house, how the seller accepted your offer for $4,000 less than you were prepared to pay, and that the ugly vinyl flooring in the master bathroom is easily replaced.

If you are prepared to experience buyer's remorse, and you know it is an entirely natural and extremely common phenomenon, you will handle it much more easily.

QUICK CHECKLIST
THE AGREEMENT OF SALE

1. Do you understand that the offer becomes the Agreement of Sale and must ultimately be signed by both the buyer and seller to be a legally binding contract?

2. Do you know that the Agreement of Sale establishes the conditions for the sale?

3. Do you realize that you must submit an earnest money deposit in some form with your offer, usually in the amount of 5 to 10% of the offered price?

4. Do you understand the clauses in the offer in the Agreement of Sale?

5. Do you realize that your offer opens the negotiations for the potential purchase of the house?

6. Have you determined a fair market price for your offer?

7. Are you prepared to negotiate on the price and/or the conditions and clauses in the Agreement of Sale?

8. Do you know that unless both parties — the buyer and the seller — agree to the sale price and the conditions for the sale, the offer is null and void and you receive your earnest money deposit back in full?

9. Do you understand that the Realtor's commission for services is paid by the seller at settlement, unless it has been established that the buyer will also have the services of a broker?

10. Do you know that more than one buyer's offer can be presented to the seller at a time and that the seller can accept the best offer, which may or may not be the highest price, but the best conditions? The seller may also reject all offers until satisfied.

11. Have you asked about zoning for this property? Is it strictly residential or could you have your business in your home?

12. Are there any deed restrictions you should know about? Ask the Realtor, if you are working with one, to get you a copy of the deed. If you are working on your own, go to the city or county courthouse and look up the deed.

13. Have you made a list of questions for your lawyer or Realtor to answer?

AGREEMENT FOR THE SALE AND PURCHASE OF REAL ESTATE

This form recommended and approved for, but not restricted to,
use by members of the Greater Harrisburg Association of REALTORS®

AGENT FOR SELLER _____   SUB AGENT FOR SELLER _____

_____ PA. LICENSED BROKER   _____ PA. LICENSED BROKER

This Agreement made this _____ day of _____, 19___.

1. PRINCIPALS Between, _____

(residing at _____
hereinafter called Seller, and

(residing at _____
hereinafter called Buyer.

2. PROPERTY: Seller hereby agrees to sell and convey to Buyer, who hereby agrees to purchase: ALL THAT CERTAIN Lot or piece of ground with buildings and improvements thereon erected, if any, known as: _____

3. ZONING: Zoning Classification _____
Failure of this Agreement to contain the zoning classification except in cases where the property (or each parcel thereof, if subdividable) is zoned solely or primarily to permit single-family dwellings shall render this Agreement voidable at the option of the Buyer and if voided deposits tendered by the Buyer shall be returned to the Buyer without a requirement of court action.

4. TERMS: (a) Purchase Price _____ ($ _____)

to be paid by the Buyer as follows:

(b) DEPOSIT Check □, Cash □, Note □ at the signing of this agreement, receipt of which is hereby acknowledged .... $ _____

If Note, to be redeemed on or before the _____ day of _____, 19___.
ADDITIONAL DEPOSIT due on or before the _____ day of _____, 19___. .... $ _____

(d) BALANCE OF PURCHASE PRICE at settlement (cash, certified check, and/or mortgage funds) .... $ _____

                                                    TOTAL .... $ _____

(e) Written approval of Seller to be on or before the _____ day of _____, 19___.
(f) Settlement to be made on or before the _____ day of _____, 19___.
(g) The following shall be apportioned pro-rata as of and at time of settlement: Taxes as levied and assessed, rents, interest on mortgage assumptions, condominium fees and homeowner association fees if any, water and/or sewer rents if any, together with any other lienable municipal services. All Realty Transfer Taxes shall be divided evenly unless otherwise provided herein.

5. PROPERTY SETTLEMENT CONTINGENCY: This agreement is subject to the settlement of Buyer's property located at _____
on or before _____

6. FINANCING CONTINGENCY: This agreement is subject to the financing as follows:

(a) PRINCIPAL AMOUNT $ _____   MAXIMUM INITIAL INTEREST RATE _____%.

TYPE _____ MINIMUM TERM _____
TERMINAL DATE for Obtaining Financing Commitment _____

Broker may advise Buyer of possible sources of mortgage funds, but cannot assume responsibility for obtaining Buyer's mortgage. If said loan cannot be obtained as herein provided, this Agreement shall be NULL AND VOID and all deposit monies shall be returned to the Buyer on or before date of settlement as provided herein, subject however to the provisions in Paragraphs 6(b) and 6(c).

(b) Buyer shall make a completed application to a responsible lending institution for the said loan within _____ days from the Seller's approval hereof. Should the Buyer fail to make such completed application within the specified time, it shall be at the option of the Seller, within five (5) days thereafter to:

(i) Declare this Agreement NULL AND VOID, at which time, all monies paid on account will be forfeited to Seller as liquidated damages, subject to the Rules and Regulations of the Pennsylvania Real Estate Commission, or

(ii) In absence of written notice to the Buyer by the Seller declaring this Agreement NULL AND VOID, the condition and contingency provided for in this Paragraph, together with any other financing contingencies that may be herein or endorsed hereto, shall no longer prevail, and this Agreement shall remain effective according to its terms in the same manner as if the condition and contingency were not a part hereof.

(c) Seller or Agent must receive a written commitment valid until the date of settlement, for the said loan, on or before the terminal date as specified. If the said commitment is not furnished with the terms as specified herein, or on other terms accepted in writing by the Buyer, on or before the specified date, Seller shall have the option, at that date, or any other time thereafter, during the term of this Agreement, until, but not beyond the date of receipt of the commitment by the Seller, or Agent, to declare this Agreement NULL AND VOID, by written notice to the Buyer of his/her decision to cancel, at which time all deposit monies paid on account shall be returned to the Buyer, subject to the payment required, if any, provided for in Paragraph 12(b): (i), (ii), and (iii).

(d) Seller hereby agrees to permit inspections by authorized appraisers, reputable certifiers and/or Buyer as may be required by the lending institution or insuring agencies.

(e) Seller hereby agrees to pay any mortgage discount points or placement fee in case of a buyer requiring VA, FHA, or conventional financing from a lending institution requiring any one or all of aforesaid fees, providing the total of said fees does not exceed _____% of the amount of the mortgage.

7. **STATUS OF WATER AND SEWER:** Seller warrants that this property is serviced by _____ water and _____ sewer. Further, Seller warrants that these systems are fully paid for and, as of the date of this agreement are in satisfactory operating condition. If aforesaid systems are private, Seller warrants that he/she has no information that public water and/or sewer will be assessed or installed for at least six (6) months after the date of settlement as aforesaid.

8. **MUNICIPAL IMPROVEMENTS:** Seller has no notices of municipal improvements (such as sidewalks, curbs, etc.) except _____ . Access to a public road may require issuance of a Highway occupancy permit from the Department of Transportation.

9. **SPECIAL CLAUSES:** _____

10. **ATTACHED ADDENDA** are made a part of this Agreement: ☐ Wood Infestation   ☐ Radon Disclosure   ☐ Private Water/Septic   ☐ Agency Relationship
☐ Other(s): _____

11. **PERSONALTY:** All existing plumbing, heating, air-conditioning and lighting fixtures (including chandeliers) and systems appurtenant thereto and forming a part thereof, and other permanent fixtures, as well as all ranges, laundry tubs, T.V. antennas, masts and rotor systems, together with wall to wall carpeting, screens, storm sash and/or doors, shades, awnings, venetian blinds, couplings for automatic washers and dryers, etc. radiator covers, cornices, water softeners, kitchen cabinets, drapery rods, drapery rod hardware, curtain rods, curtain rod hardware, all trees, shrubbery, plantings now in or on property, garage door openers, sheds; if any, unless specifically excepted in this Agreement, are included in the sale and purchase price. None of the above mentioned items shall be removed or substituted by the Seller from premises after date of this Agreement. Any remaining heating and/or cooking fuels stored on the premises at time of settlement are also included under this Agreement. Seller hereby warrants that he/she will deliver good title to all of the articles described in this paragraph, and any other fixtures or items of personalty specifically scheduled to be included in this sale. Seller warrants all plumbing, heating, air conditioning, mechanical and electrical systems and equipment and appliances to be in proper working order at time of settlement. This warranty does not survive closing.

[Do Not Write in This Space]

12. TITLE AND COSTS:

(a) The premises are to be conveyed in fee simple by special warranty deed, free and clear of all liens, encumbrances and easements, EXCEPTING HOWEVER, the following: Existing building restrictions, ordinances, easements of roads, privileges or rights of public service companies, if any; or easements or restrictions visible upon the ground, otherwise the title to the above described real estate shall be good and marketable or such as will be insured by a reputable title insurance company at the regular rates.

(b) The Buyer will pay for the following:
   (i)   The premium for title insurance, mechanics lien insurance and/or title search, or fee for cancellation of same, if any.
   (ii) The premium for flood insurance and/or fire insurance with extended coverage, insurance binder charges or cancellation fee, if any.
   (iii) Appraisal fees and charges paid in advance to mortgagee, if any.
   (iv) Buyer's normal settlement costs and accruals unless otherwise stated herein.

(c) Any survey or surveys which may be required by the Title Insurance Company or the abstracting attorney for the preparation of an adequate legal description of the premises (or the correction thereof), shall be secured and paid for by the Seller. However, any survey or surveys desired by the Buyer or required by his mortgagee shall be secured and paid for by the Buyer.

(d) In the event the Seller is unable to give a good and marketable title or such as will be insured by a reputable title insurance company, subject as aforesaid, Buyer shall have the option of taking such title as the Seller can give without abatement of price or of being repaid all monies paid by the Buyer to the Seller on account of the purchase price and the Seller will reimburse the Buyer for any costs incurred by the Buyer for those items specified in Paragraph 12(b) items (i), (ii), (iii) and in Paragraph 12(c); and in the latter event there shall be no further liability or objection on either of the parties hereto and this Agreement shall become NULL AND VOID.

13. PAYMENT OF DEPOSIT:
Deposits, regardless of the form of payment and the person designated as payee, shall be paid to Agent for the Seller, who shall retain them in an escrow account until consummation or termination of this Agreement in conformity with all applicable laws and regulations. Agent for the Seller may, at his or her sole option, hold any uncashed check tendered as deposit, pending the acceptance of this offer.

If there is a dispute between the Buyer and the Seller over who is entitled to the deposit, Agent will not be responsible to resolve that dispute and will not be liable to either Buyer or the Seller for refusing to release the deposit without an adequate written agreement between Buyer and Seller or a valid court order. Buyer and Seller agree that, in the event the Agent and/or Subagent are/is joined in litigation for the return of deposit monies, the Agent's and/or Subagent's reasonable attorney's fees and costs will be paid by the party joining the Agent or Subagent.

14. POSSESSION AND TENDER:

(a) Possession is to be delivered by deed, keys and physical possession to a vacant building (if any) at day and time of settlement, or by deed and assignment of existing lease(s) at the time of settlement if premises is tenant occupied at the signing of this Agreement, unless otherwise specified herein. Buyer will acknowledge existing lease(s) by initialing said lease(s) at time of signing of this Agreement of Sale if tenant occupied.

(b) Seller will not enter into any new lease(s), written extension of existing lease(s), if any, or additional lease(s) for the premises without express written consent of the Buyer.

(c) Formal tender of an executed deed and purchase money is hereby waived.

(d) Buyer reserves the right to make a presettlement inspection of the subject premises, and will execute appropriate documentation of such inspection.

15. RISK OF LOSS:

(a) Seller shall maintain the property (including all items mentioned in paragraph #11 herein) and any personal property specifically scheduled herein in its present condition, normal wear and tear excepted.

(b) Seller shall bear risk of loss from fire or other casualty until time of settlement. In the event of damage to the property by fire or other casualty, Buyer shall have the option of rescinding this agreement and receiving hand money paid on account of accepting the property in its then condition with the proceeds of any insurance recovery obtainable by Seller. Buyer is hereby notified that he may insure his equitable interest in this property as of the time of the acceptance of this agreement.

16. REPRESENTATIONS:
It is understood that Buyer has inspected the property, or hereby waives the right to do so and he/she has agreed to purchase it as a result of such inspection and not because of or in reliance upon any representation made by the Seller or any other officer, partner or employee of Seller, or by the agent of the Seller or in its present condition unless otherwise specified herein and further acknowledges that the aforementioned parties are not qualified to render an opinion on construction, engineering, or environmental matters and that the buyer has been advised that he/she may require or wish to seek the assistance of experts in those fields. It is further understood that this Agreement contains the whole agreement between the Seller and Buyer and there are no other terms, obligations, covenants, representations, statements or conditions, oral or otherwise of any kind whatsoever concerning this sale. Furthermore, this Agreement shall not be altered, amended, changed or modified except in writing executed by the parties hereto.

17. RECORDING:
This agreement shall not be recorded in the Office for the Recording of Deeds or in any other office or place of public record, and if Buyer shall record this agreement or cause or permit the same to be recorded, Seller may, at his/her option, elect to treat such act as a breach of this agreement.

18. ASSIGNMENT:
This Agreement shall be binding upon the respective heirs, executors, administrators, successors and, to the extent assignable, on the assigns of the parties hereto, it being expressly understood, however, that the Buyer shall not transfer or assign this Agreement without the written consent of the Seller being first obtained.

19. NON-LIABILITY OF AGENT:
Except as may be provided by an addendum to this Agreement, Agent(s) or Sub-Agent(s), if any, are representing Seller, not the Buyer. It is expressly understood and agreed between the parties hereto that the herein named agent, his/her salespersons and employees or any officer or partner or agent and any cooperating broker and his/her salespersons and employees and any officer or partner of the cooperating broker are acting as agent only in bringing the Buyer and Seller together, and will in no case whatsoever be held liable jointly or severally to either party for the performance of any item or covenant of this Agreement or for damages for the nonperformance thereof.

20. DEFAULT – TIME IS OF THE ESSENCE:
The said time for settlement and all other items referred to for the performance of any of the obligations of this Agreement are hereby agreed to be of the essence of this Agreement. Should the Buyer:

(a) Fail to make any additional payments as specified in Paragraph 4,

(b) Furnish false or incomplete information to the Seller, the Seller's agent, or the mortgage lender, concerning the Buyer's legal or financial status, or fail to cooperate in the processing of the mortgage loan application, which acts would result in the failure to obtain the approval of a mortgage loan commitment, or

(c) Violate or fail to fulfill and perform any of the terms or conditions of this Agreement, then in such case, all deposit monies and other sums paid by the Buyer on account of the purchase price, whether required by this Agreement or not, may be retained;
   (i)   by the Seller on account of the purchase price, should the seller demand the full purchase price, or
   (ii) as monies to be applied to the Seller's damages, or
   (iii) as liquidated damages for such breach,

as the Seller may elect, and in the event that the Seller elects to retain the monies as liquidated damages in accordance with Paragraph 20(c)(iii), the Seller shall be released from all liability or obligation as this Agreement shall be NULL AND VOID.

21. **RECOVERY FUND:** A real estate recovery fund exists to reimburse any persons who has obtained a final civil judgment against a Pennsylvania real estate licensee owing to fraud, misrepresentation, or deceit in a real estate transaction and who has been unable to collect the judgement after exhausting all legal and equitable remedies. For complete details about the fund, call (717) 783-3658.

22. **DESCRIPTIVE HEADING:** The descriptive headings used herein are for convenience only and they are not intended to indicate all of the matter in the sections which follow them. Accordingly, they shall have no effect whatsoever in determining the rights or obligations of the parties.

23. **AGREEMENT:** THIS AGREEMENT CONTAINS THE WHOLE AGREEMENT BETWEEN THE SELLER AND BUYER. THERE ARE NO OTHER TERMS, OBLIGATIONS, COVENANTS, REPRESENTATIONS, STATEMENTS OR CONDITIONS, ORAL OR OTHERWISE, OF ANY KIND WHATSOEVER CONCERNING THIS SALE, EXCEPT AS ATTACHED TO THIS CONTRACT.

[Do Not Write in This Space]

This is a legally binding contract; if not understood, consult your attorney.

Fax Statement: This Document and any amendments thereto, may be executed in multiple counterparts by the parties and delivered by way of transmission through a facsimile (FAX) machine and such counterparts shall have the same legal enforceability and binding effect as though it were signed by all parties in original form.

APPROVAL BY BUYER: In witness whereof, the parties hereto, intending to be legally bound hereby, have hereunder set their hands and seals the day and year first above written.

_____ BUYER _____ (SEAL)

_____ BUYER _____ (SEAL)

WITNESS AS TO BUYER

WITNESS AS TO BUYER

APPROVAL BY SELLER: Seller(s) hereby approves contract this _____ day of _____, 19___.

_____ SELLER _____ (SEAL)

_____ SELLER _____ (SEAL)

WITNESS AS TO SELLER

AGENT BY: _____   HSA #6   5/91

Agreement of Sale
By permission of Greater Harrisburg Association of Realtors, 1992.

PRIVATE WATER/SEPTIC ADDENDUM TO AGREEMENT OF SALE

This form recommended and approved for, but not restricted to, use by members of the Greater Harrisburg Association of REALTORS®.

DATE OF SALES AGREEMENT: _____ SETTLEMENT DATE: _____

RE: PROPERTY: _____

SELLER(S): _____

BUYER(S): _____

I. STATEMENTS (A) _____ and/or (B) _____ (Check one or both.)

A. PRIVATE WATER POTABILITY TEST (Check one)

☐ Prior to settlement, SELLER(S) shall, at: ☐ BUYER(S)' expense or ☐ SELLER(S)' expense, order from a Water Testing Laboratory certified by the Pennsylvania Department of Environmental Resources (PA-DER), a written report.

This report shall contain: (Check one)

☐ A bacteriological analysis   ☐ A bacteriological and chemical analysis

which shall be in compliance with mortgage and lending institution requirements and/or Federal Insuring and Guaranteeing Agency requirements, if any. Said report shall be presented to the BUYER(S) promptly upon receipt. Such a report is to provide that the water is within the Maximum Contamination Levels (MCL's) as established by the Pennsylvania Department of Environmental Resources.

If the report reveals that the water is not within the said DER MCL's, the SELLER(S) within five (5) days of receipt of said report shall advise whether water supply will be treated to comply with DER standards at SELLER(S) expense by purchase of appropriate equipment prior to settlement. If SELLER(S) elects not to treat the water source, BUYER(S) shall have the option of: 1) accepting the property with the water not potable as revealed by said report and agrees to the release set forth below in **II. RELEASE**; or 2) being repaid all monies paid by the BUYER(S) on account of the purchase price, together with BUYER(S)' expenses, if any, as may be incurred or provided for under the terms of the Agreement of Sale, including but not limited to the following:

A. Cancellation fee for title insurance or abstract fee for searching title;

B. Cancellation fee or binder charge for fire insurance with extended coverage and/or flood insurance, if any;

C. Appraisal fees, credit report charges and/or survey costs; and

D. Water testing fees.

In the latter event, there shall be no further liability or obligation on either of the parties hereto, and this Agreement of Sale shall become NULL AND VOID. BUYER(S) shall notify SELLER(S) in writing of option within five (5) days after BUYER(S) receives SELLER(S) notice of refusal to take remedial action.

SELLER(S) warrants that SELLER(S) own all equipment associated with the water system, except _____

☐ BUYER(S) waive testing of said water. BUYER(S) further acknowledge that no statements have been made to them by any parties to this transaction regarding the potability or chemical content of the water provided to subject property. BUYER(S) herein acknowledge that BUYER(S) have been informed that subject property has a private well for its water source and advised to have the well water tested by a Water Testing Laboratory. BUYER(S) agrees to the release as set forth below in **II. RELEASE.**

B. PRIVATE ON-LOT SEWAGE SYSTEM (Check one)

☐ Prior to settlement, SELLER(S) shall, at: ☐ BUYER(S)' expense or ☐ SELLER(S)' expense, have private on-lot sewage system opened, the tank pumped and inspected by a reputable septic company and provide to the SELLER(S) promptly upon receipt an inspection report. Said report shall be in compliance with applicable laws, mortgage and lending institution requirements and/or Federal Insuring and Guaranteeing Agency requirements, if any. Should report reveal defects in the system, the SELLER(S) within five (5) days of receipt of said report, shall advise BUYER(S), in writing, whether repairs will be made at SELLER(S)' expense prior to settlement.

If SELLER(S) elects not to make the repairs, BUYER shall have the option of: 1) accepting the property with the system defects as revealed by the report and agrees to the release as set forth below in **II. RELEASE**; or 2) being repaid all monies paid by the BUYER(S) on account of the purchase price, together with BUYER(S)' expenses, if any, as may be incurred or provided for under the terms of the Agreement of Sale, including but not limited to the following:

A. Cancellation fee for title insurance or abstract fee for searching title;
B. Cancellation fee or binder charge for fire insurance with extended coverage and/or flood insurance, if any;
C. Appraisal fees, credit report charges, and/or survey costs; and
D. Private on-lot sewage Inspection fees.

In the latter event, there shall be no further liability or obligation on either of the parties hereto, and this Agreement of Sale shall become NULL AND VOID. BUYER(S) shall notify SELLER(S) in writing of option within five (5) days after BUYER(S) receives SELLER(S) notice of refusal to take remedial action.

☐ BUYER(S) waive testing of said on-lot sewage system. BUYER(S) further acknowledge that no statements have been made to them by any parties to this transaction regarding the condition of said system. BUYER(S) herein acknowledge that BUYER(S) have been informed that subject property has a private on-lot sewage system and advised to have the said system inspected by a reputable septic company. BUYER(S) agrees to the release as set forth below in **II. RELEASE.**

SELLER(S) certifies that there has been no history of problems with the on-lot sewage system except _____

II. RELEASE

The Buyer(s) hereby release, quit claims and forever discharges Seller(s), Seller(s) agents, subagents, employees and any officer or partner or any of them and any other person, firm or corporation who may be liable by or through them, from any and all claims, losses or demands, including personal injuries, and all the consequences thereof, where now known or not, which may arise from results found in the water potability test and/or the private on-lot sewage system inspection.

Fax Statement: This Document and any amendments thereto, may be executed in multiple counterparts by the parties and delivered by way of transmission through a facsimile (FAX) machine and such counterparts shall have the same legal enforceability and binding effect as though it were signed by all parties in original form.

WITNESS: _____ DATE _____ BUYER(S): _____ (SEAL)

WITNESS: _____ DATE _____ BUYER(S): _____ (SEAL)

WITNESS: _____ DATE _____ SELLER(S): _____ (SEAL)

WITNESS: _____ DATE _____ SELLER(S): _____ (SEAL)

HWS #3 8/91

Addendum Example
By permission of Greater Harrisburg Association of Realtors, 1989.

RADON DISCLOSURE ADDENDUM
TO EXCLUSIVE RIGHT TO SELL AND AGREEMENT OF SALE

This form recommended and approved for, but not restricted to, use by members of the Greater Harrisburg Association of REALTORS®

DATE OF LISTING: _____, 19___ DATE OF SALES AGREEMENT: _____, 19___ SETTLEMENT DATE: _____, 19___

RE: PROPERTY: _____

SELLER(S): _____   BUYER(S): _____

NOTICE TO SELLER(S)/BUYER(S) REGARDING RADON GAS

1. Radon has always been present in the air; consequently varying levels of radon gas may be found in virtually all homes.

2. Radon is a radioactive gas produced naturally in the ground by the normal decay of uranium and radium. Uranium and radium are widely distributed in trace amounts in the earth's crust. Descendents of Radon gas are called Radon daughters, or Radon progeny. Several Radon daughters emit alpha radiation, which has high energy but short range.

3. Studies indicate the result of extended exposure to high levels of Radon gas/Radon daughters, may be an increased risk of lung cancer.

4. Radon gas originates in soil and rocks. It diffuses, as does any gas, and flows along the path of least resistance to the surface of the ground and then to the atmosphere. Being a gas, Radon can also move into any air space, such as basements, crawl spaces and living areas.

5. If a house has a Radon problem, it can usually be cured by (a) increased ventilation and/or (b) preventing Radon entry.

6. The EPA advises corrective action if the Annual average exposure to Radon daughters exceeds 4 picocuries/liter. EPA further advises that in most cases, the short term screening measurement is NOT a reliable measure of the annual average radon level of exposure. If the short term screening measurement result is 4 picocuries/liter to 20 picocuries/liter, follow-up measurements to determine an annual average are recommended.

7. Further information can be secured from the DER Radon Office, P.O. Box 2063, Harrisburg, PA 17120; Call 1-800-23RADON or (717) 783-3594.

RADON DISCLOSURE/EXCLUSIVE RIGHT TO SELL

1. SELLER(S) hereby acknowledges receipt of notice as set forth above and certifies that (check only one):

a. ( ) The property had ☐ Short term screening ☐ Annual testing ☐ Other _____

testing by: ☐ SELLER(S) ☐ Certified Testing services on _____

The results of which were: _____ picocuries/liter.

( ) In addition, SELLER(S) took remedial action on _____

and the radon was reduced to _____ picocuries/liter.

b. ( ) SELLER(S) have no knowledge concerning the presence or absence or Radon.

2. SELLER(S) hereby authorize agent and any subagents, to disclose the foregoing information to prospective buyers.

WITNESS: _____   SELLER(S): _____

WITNESS: _____   SELLER(S): _____

RADON DISCLOSURE/AGREEMENT OF SALE

1. BUYER(S) acknowledges receipt of notice as set forth above.

2. **BUYER(S) OPTION** (Check only one):

   a. ( ) BUYER(S) acknowledges he has the right to have the building(s) inspected to determine if Radon gas/daughters is present. BUYER(S) waive this right and agree to accept property and agrees to the release set forth below, in item 3, RELEASE.

   b. ( ) BUYER(S) acknowledge results of SELLER(S) certification at _____ picocuries/liter and agrees to accept property and agrees to the release set forth below in item 3, RELEASE.

   c. ( ) BUYER(S) at BUYER(S) expense shall secure and provide a written radon report from a certified radon testing firm on the property on or before _____. Failure of BUYER to produce the report to SELLER within the time herein specified shall constitute a waiver of BUYER'S right to a radon contingency. Upon such waiver, BUYER agrees to accept the property and agrees to the release set forth below, in item #3, RELEASE.
   At the time of said notice to the SELLER(S), SELLER(S) shall advise whether or not the level of radon detected will be corrected at SELLER(S) expense, prior to settlement, if the level exceeds _____ picocuries/liter.
   If SELLER(S) elects to take remedial action at SELLER(S) expense, the remaining provisions of this contract remain unaltered and BUYER(S) agrees to the release as set forth below in item 3, RELEASE.
   If SELLER(S) elects not to take the remedial action, if any, BUYER(S) shall have the option of: 1) accepting the property with the radon levels revealed by the testing, without abatement of price and agrees to the release set forth below in item 3, RELEASE, or 2) being repaid all monies paid by the BUYER(S) on account of the purchase price, together with BUYER(S) expenses, if any, as may be incurred or provided for under the terms of the Agreement of Sale, including but not limited to the following:

   A. Cancellation fee for title insurance or abstract fee for searching title.
   B. Cancellation fee or binder charge for fire insurance with extended coverage and/or flood insurance if any.
   C. Appraisal fees, credit report charges, and/or survey costs.
   In the latter event, there shall be no further liability or obligation on either of the parties hereto, and this Agreement of Sale shall become **NULL AND VOID**. BUYER(S) shall notify SELLER(S) in writing of option within five (5) days after BUYER(S) receives SELLER(S) notice of refusal to take remedial action.

3. **RELEASE**
   The BUYER(S) hereby releases, quit claims and forever discharges SELLER(S), SELLER(S) AGENTS, SUBAGENTS, EMPLOYEES and any OFFICER or PARTNER or any one of them and any other PERSON, FIRM, or CORPORATION, who may be liable by or through them, from any and all claims, losses or demands, including personal injuries, and all of the consequences thereof, where now known or not, which may arise from the presence of Radon in any buildings on the property.

   Fax Statement: This Document and any amendments thereto, may be executed in multiple counterparts by the parties and delivered by way of transmission through a facsimile (FAX) machine and such counterparts shall have the same legal enforceability and binding effect as though it were signed by all parties in original form.

   WITNESS: _____   BUYER(S): _____   DATE: _____

   WITNESS: _____   BUYER(S): _____   DATE: _____

   WITNESS: _____   SELLER(S): _____   DATE: _____

   WITNESS: _____   SELLER(S): _____   DATE: _____

HRD #4 3/91

Addendum Example
By permission of Greater Harrisburg Association of Realtors, 1989.

WOOD INFESTATION ADDENDUM
TO AGREEMENT OF SALE

This form recommended and approved for, but not restricted to, use by members of the Greater Harrisburg Association of REALTORS® .

DATE OF SALES AGREEMENT: _____, 19_____   SETTLEMENT DATE: _____, 19_____

RE: PROPERTY: _____

SELLER(S): _____   BUYER(S): _____

1. Prior to settlement, SELLER(S) shall at: [   ] BUYER(S) or [   ] SELLER(S) expense, order from a Pest Control Operator certified by the Pennsylvania Department of Agriculture a written "Wood Destroying Insect Infestation and Resultant Damage Report" and shall present said report to all other parties to the Agreement. Such report is to provide that an inspection of the readily visible and accessible area of all structures within the property limits has been made satisfactory to and in compliance with applicable laws, mortgage and lending institutions, and/or Federal Insuring and Guaranteeing Agency requirements, if any.

2. Seller shall, upon receipt of said report, promptly provide a copy of the complete report to all parties to the Agreement.

   If the inspection reveals evidence of active infestation(s) and/or previous investation(s) which has not been corrected, SELLER(S) agree, at SELLER(S) expense to have the structure(s) treated for such infestation. Exceptions, if any:
   _____

3. At the time of notice as specified above in paragraph 2, SELLER(S) shall also advise within five (5) days whether or not the resultant structural damage, if any, will be repaired, at SELLER(S) expense, prior to settlement. If SELLER(S) elect not to repair such damage, BUYER(S) shall have the option of accepting the property with the defects revealed by the inspection, without abatement of price, or being repaid all monies paid by the BUYER(S) on account of the purchase price, together with BUYER(S) expenses, if any, as may be incurred or provided for under the terms of the Agreement of Sale, including but not limited to the following:
   A. Cancellation fee for title insurance or abstract fee for searching title.
   B. Cancellation fee or binder charge for fire insurance with extended coverage and/or flood insurance, if any.
   C. Appraisal fees, credit report charges, and/or survey costs.

   In the latter event, there should be no further liability or obligation on either of the parties hereto and this Agreement of Sale shall become **NULL AND VOID.** BUYER(S) shall notify SELLER(S) of his election within five (5) days after BUYER(S) receives SELLER(S) notice of refusal to correct the condition(s).

All other terms and conditions of the said Agreement shall remain unchanged and in full force and effect.

FAX STATEMENT: This Document and any amendments thereto, may be executed in multiple counterparts by the parties and delivered by way of transmission through a facsimile (FAX) machine and such counterparts shall have the same legal enforceabily and binding effect as though it were signed by all parties in their original form.

WITNESS: _____ BUYER: _____ DATE:_____

WITNESS: _____ BUYER: _____ DATE:_____

WITNESS: _____ SELLER: _____ DATE:_____

WITNESS: _____ SELLER: _____ DATE:_____

Addendum Example
By permission of Greater Harrisburg Association of Realtors, 1989.

— 10 —

Inspection

Peter bought his first house at a tax sale. He checked on the amount of back taxes, utilities, and liens. He took the time to view the property quickly before he submitted his sealed bid. Peter was not experienced at inspecting a property for possible structural problems. When he went through the property, it looked okay to him, even though it was rundown. He was awarded the house. After he settled on his bargain house, he took some friends to see it. It had rained recently. As they walked through the house, Peter found a basement floor covered with water, a ceiling crack dripping steadily, and a strong, musty smell permeating the house. What serious problems could Peter be faced with in this house?

Continuous water on the walls and joints could cause rot and crumbling of plaster throughout the house. Long-term neglect of these types of problems can lead to the weakening of foundations, roofs, and walls. Peter was in such a hurry to buy this house that he forgot to inspect it carefully.

Have you checked the house that you want to buy for its structural soundness? It is well worth getting a professional inspection. Although professional inspections run several hundred dollars it is almost always money well spent. Even if the inspector finds absolutely nothing to question, your peace of mind is worth the investment.

What is structural soundness? You will want to know that the roof, walls, and foundation of your house are sound. You must be sure you will be safe from collapse or damage caused by unsafe structures. Long-term neglect of water damage from leaking roofs, leaking basements, cracked interior and exterior walls, and infestation of wood joists and floors by termites and other destructive insects are the major causes of severe structural weakness. Sometimes you will not be able to see cracked walls if paneling and siding have been used on the house. It is these serious problems that you as the buyer must be sure to check out. Remember, buyer beware!

PROFESSIONAL INSPECTION

Standards are set for home inspections by the American Society of Home Inspectors (A.S.H.I.). This group has approximately 500 members throughout the fifty states. Check in your telephone book for a local group. An excellent resource to give you some background material and an idea of what a professional inspector is looking for is *The Home Buyer's Inspection Guide*, by James Madorma (Betterway, 1990).

If you decide to have the property inspected by a professional, first you must find the person to do the inspection. Your Realtor may be able to recommend someone. Look in the telephone book yellow pages under "Building Inspection Service." Ask the inspectors you speak to for references on previous jobs.

If you included an inspection contingency in the Agreement of Sale, presumably there was a time frame in which this had to be completed (usually just a couple of days). You will need to contact a professional inspector, and get your Realtor to make an appointment with the seller to do the inspection. You should definitely plan to accompany the inspector when he or she inspects the property. The inspector may not say a whole lot while he is doing the inspection, depending on whether or not the seller is present. He should provide a complete written report of his findings. (Ask about this in advance. If you do not have a written report, you won't have a leg to stand on when you approach the seller about repairs.) The inspection should cover all the areas mentioned in the following chart.

EXTERIOR

FOUNDATION
- ❏ Minor cracks
- ❏ Settlement cracks
- ❏ Bulging walls

SIDING
- ❏ Brick, stucco, or mortar failure
- ❏ Caulking
- ❏ Aluminum or vinyl siding dented, loose, missing
- ❏ Wood siding rotted, damaged, missing
- ❏ Asbestos siding damaged
- ❏ Painting needed on siding or trim

ROOF
- ❏ Age of roofing material
- ❏ Asphalt shingles damaged or worn
- ❏ More than two layers of asphalt shingles
- ❏ Slate roof worn, nails failing
- ❏ Wood shingles damaged or worn
- ❏ Water puddles
- ❏ Chimney leaning or damaged
- ❏ Flashing needed

GUTTERS AND DOWNSPOUTS
- ❏ Age of gutters and downspouts
- ❏ Condition of gutters and downspouts
- ❏ Condition of fascia board
- ❏ Concrete slab or splash block needed

DOORS
- ❏ Doors damaged, need refinishing or replacement
- ❏ Locks not working
- ❏ Weatherstripping needed
- ❏ Jambs damaged, need refinishing or replacement
- ❏ Storm door needed

WINDOWS
- ❏ Wood needs painting
- ❏ Sashes or sills damaged, need refinishing or replacement
- ❏ Broken glass
- ❏ Locks not working
- ❏ Storm windows or energy-efficient windows needed

DRIVEWAY/WALKWAY
- ❏ Blacktop cracked or damaged
- ❏ Concrete cracked or damaged
- ❏ Tree roots encroaching

GARAGE
- ❏ Concrete floor cracked
- ❏ Door needs refinishing or replacement
- ❏ Automatic door opener needs repair

INTERIOR

FRAMING
- ❏ Type of framing (platform or balloon)
- ❏ Sill plate damaged
- ❏ Evidence of termite infestation
- ❏ Subflooring damaged
- ❏ Condition of main beam

BASEMENT
- ❏ Evidence of water entry
- ❏ Ventilation poor

LIVING ROOM
- ❏ Outlets not working
- ❏ Walls, ceiling cracked
- ❏ Drywall failing
- ❏ Flooring damaged
- ❏ Carpeting damaged
- ❏ Water stains near windows
- ❏ Fireplace not functional or unsafe

DINING ROOM
- ❏ Outlets not working
- ❏ Walls, ceiling cracked
- ❏ Drywall failing
- ❏ Flooring damaged
- ❏ Carpeting damaged
- ❏ Water stains near windows

KITCHEN
- ❏ Ground-fault interrupter outlets needed
- ❏ Walls, ceiling cracked
- ❏ Drywall failing
- ❏ Flooring damaged
- ❏ Sink damaged
- ❏ Leaking faucet, trap
- ❏ Water pressure, drainage inadequate
- ❏ Cabinets need refinishing, hardware, or replacement
- ❏ Countertop stained, worn, or damaged
- ❏ Appliances malfunctioning (if included in sale)

STAIRWAYS
- ❏ Risers, treads damaged
- ❏ Handrail, newel post loose
- ❏ Carpeting damaged

BEDROOMS
- ❏ Outlets not working
- ❏ Walls, ceiling cracked
- ❏ Drywall failing
- ❏ Flooring damaged
- ❏ Carpeting damaged
- ❏ Water stains near windows

BATHROOMS
- ❏ Ground-fault interrupter outlets needed
- ❏ Tiles loose or cracked
- ❏ Flooring damaged
- ❏ Sink damaged
- ❏ Water pressure, drainage inadequate
- ❏ Ceiling damaged
- ❏ Faucet, trap leaking
- ❏ Toilet leaking, cracked, or chipped
- ❏ Tub leaking, cracked, or chipped
- ❏ Grout missing
- ❏ Shower stall pan leaking
- ❏ Shower door leaking
- ❏ Water stains on ceiling below bathroom

ATTIC
- ❏ Insulation needed
- ❏ Ventilation needed
- ❏ Attic fan needed
- ❏ Evidence of water entry
- ❏ Stairs or access to attic unsafe

Systems

PLUMBING
- ❏ Type of piping
- ❏ Pipes leaking
- ❏ Pipe insulation needed
- ❏ Water quality checked (call National Testing Laboratories at 800-458-3330).
- ❏ Well not functioning properly
- ❏ Septic tank needs to be pumped

ELECTRICAL
- ❏ New circuit breaker box or fuse box needed
- ❏ Outlets, switches damaged
- ❏ Wiring old, needs replacement
- ❏ Ground-fault interrupter outlets needed

HEATING/AIR CONDITIONING
- ❏ Type of furnace, boiler, or heat pump
- ❏ Heating system needs cleaning, repair
- ❏ Type of air conditioning
- ❏ Air conditioning system needs cleaning, repair

Alternatives to Professional Inspection

If you determine that you do not want a professional inspection, do so at your own risk. There are few substitutes for the training a professional inspector has to offer. However, if you do not go that route, you may want to ask a general contractor whose opinion you trust to go over the house with you. There are also a number of home inspection books on the market that could help you do your own inspection. Please keep in mind that a professional home inspector knows exactly what to look for: would you know a cracked heat exchanger in a furnace if you saw one?

CODE VIOLATIONS AND ZONING LAWS

In some places, the local government requires a checklist of code violations for each house bought or sold. Usually these specifications focus on safety hazards and require that code violations be fixed and brought into compliance. If such a list is available, you should request a copy. It is very helpful to get an idea of what needs to be done to the property before you buy.

If the property you are interested in is located in a designated historic district, you will encounter special restrictions and requirements. Be sure to check out all those requirements as well as the zoning laws. Remember that zoning is important to you. Zoning by the local government is a way to protect residential neighborhoods from homeowners doing whatever they want with the property. For example, without zoning laws your neighbor might decide to put in an unacceptable business enterprise, or build a high-rise apartment complex, or develop a go-cart track, or whatever. Commercial, industrial, and business zones are designated for these reasons. Professional offices in some residential areas are permitted. Check the zoning to be sure of the restrictions before you buy a house.

QUICK CHECKLIST INSPECTIONS

1. Do you know what to look for in a house to determine its structural integrity?

2. Does the local government require a code violation inspection?

3. Did your contract include an inspection addendum?

4. Have you contacted a professional inspector and arranged (with your Realtor) for the inspection?

5. Has the property been tested for radon, termites, water leaks, lead, asbestos, and other threats to the property's safety? The Environmental Assessment Association may be able to offer some guidance here (602) 483-8100.

6. Did you investigate the surrounding area for possible hazards? The Citizen's Clearing House for Hazardous Wastes, 119 Rowell Court, P.O. Box 6806, Falls Church, VA 22040 can send to you a neighborhood "Toxic Report."

7. Have you had a report on possible insect infestation?

— 11 —
Financing

Beth was unprepared for the experience of applying for a mortgage. When she was married, her husband had taken care of all those kinds of things; she just signed the papers. She heard a radio ad from a local bank declaring that they had mortgage money. She called and set up an appointment with the loan officer since she had a signed Agreement of Sale on the house she wanted to buy. But when she got to her appointment, it soon became obvious that she did not have the answers to the questions needed to complete the application process. She had not done her homework and was not prepared. This meant that she had to reschedule her appointment and hope that her loan request could be processed within the time frame agreed to in the Agreement of Sale. What should Beth have taken with her to the appointment with the loan officer to have avoided this setback?

Beth needs to have proof of employment (a recent pay-check stub), tax records (a copy of the last two years' federal income tax return), a statement of her net worth, a list of outstanding debts (include account numbers and locations of accounts and loans), the signed Agreement of Sale, and her checkbook for this meeting. If, after the loan officer takes the information for the application, more documentation is needed, Beth will be able to complete the application to get the process in motion and get the other documentation to the lender in the following days. Also, in her haste, Beth had not compared lenders for terms, rates, and services.

The process of buying a home is now moving along, but the hurdle ahead is a significant one. Finding a financing source or mortgage lender in today's markets is very challenging indeed. Shop around. Ask pertinent questions of potential lenders. Have a good idea where you want to do business when the time comes.

Often, if you are working with a Realtor, he will know which local lenders have favorable rates and are interested in residential mortgages. His tips here can save you a lot of time. Sometimes a Realtor has worked with the lender over the years and has established a good working relationship. The Realtor will often recommend you to the loan officer. All these services are valuable when looking for a financing source.

The financial institutions most commonly available to you are:

- Commercial bank — An institution for savings, loans, checking accounts, and other services, not all of which are found in savings and loan institutions. Banks are generally more active in construction loans than in long-term real estate financing.
- Savings and loan association — Originally an association chartered to hold savings and make real estate loans, federally insured and regulated. Active in long-term financing rather than construction loans. Some offer checking and other services.
- Mutual savings bank — An institution owned by its depositors as evidenced by certificates of deposit rather than stock. These institutions are active in long-term real estate financing.

- Mortgage banking company — Company providing mortgage financing with its own funds rather than simply bringing together lender and borrower, as does a mortgage broker. Usually these companies sell the mortgages to investors, and often to insurance companies.
- Mortgage broker — A person who, for a fee, brings together a borrower and a lender and does the paperwork for the borrower.

WHAT A LENDER LOOKS FOR IN A BUYER

When you strike out to find a mortgage on your own, you will discover that lenders, like insurance companies, are happy to serve you when you pose little risk. You will be faced with a tough challenge. You will have to look like a very stable, strong, low-risk buyer. How will you do this?

- It is important that you know what you are doing.
- You must be employed or be able to show five years' income tax history if you are self-employed.
- You should have a low debt-to-income ratio.
- You should dress neatly and be professional and informed in your approach with the loan officer.
- You will have to give the loan officer a feeling of confidence in you.
- You will need to have between 5 and 20% down payment in savings for the purchase and enough monthly income to carry the mortgage loan payments. You will also need to prove you have enough money for closing costs and one or two months' mortgage payments.

You may qualify for special low interest government-guaranteed mortgages for inner-city housing programs. If you are a veteran, a VA loan may be available to you. These programs are usually managed by banks, savings and loans, city housing departments, or other financial lenders. Ask about the choices they may have for you as a single person.

LENDERS VARY

You should interview at least three lending companies before you make a formal application for your mortgage. You will interview them regarding their fees, rates, terms, programs, and requirements for a mortgage loan. Each institution has one or more loan officers to serve you. Make an appointment with the loan officer who handles residential mortgages at each of the companies you are interested in doing business with at this time. Ask questions. Tell them what you would like to do and how much you intend to borrow.

Consider the chart below. Which lender would you choose?

You will see that the financing sources vary. The terms, rates, and points, in addition to the application fees, will differ. Take time to understand what these figures will mean to you over time. For example, if your mortgage is for thirty years at a fixed rate, you will pay the same base amount every

COMPARING LENDERS		
	Lender 1	Lender 2	Lender 3
Term	Interest Rate (points)	Interest Rate (points)	Interest Rate (points)
30 year fixed	8.25 (2.50)	8.50 (2.50)	9.00 (2)
15 year fixed	7.75 (2.75)	8.00 (2.50)	8.50 (2)
30 year ARM	5.50 (3.50)	6.75 (2.50)	7.00 (2)
Application fee	$275	$300	$265

month during the time you have the mortgage. (The actual amount you pay may change based on changes in your property taxes and insurance if these charges are included as part of your mortgage.) But if your mortgage is a thirty-year ARM (Adjustable Rate Mortgage), you will pay different monthly payments adjusted yearly during the time you have the mortgage unless otherwise stated.

POINTS AND CLOSING COSTS

A point equals 1% of the loan amount. Take, for example, a mortgage loan for $85,000 at an interest rate of 7.5% with 3.25 points to pay. The amount of money you would pay in points would be $2,762.50 for this loan. In general, points are fully tax deductible. Consult with your accountant or mortgage lender for details.

The application fee is a one-time charge and generally includes the property appraisal, the credit report, document preparation, and recording fees. It is possible that your application fee with various services could be $675 and would be collected from you at your application meeting. A personal check is accepted for this part of the transaction.

PMI, or Private Mortgage Insurance, is (as mentioned earlier) insurance the bank takes out on you in case you default on the loan. In general, the bank will charge PMI until you have 20% equity in the home. If you make a 20% down payment (assuming the bank's appraisal is in line with your contract

price), PMI may be waived. Check with your lender for the charge for PMI and its terms.

Be sure to know the conditions of the loan. Remember too that, as a rule of thumb, you will have to live in your home from three to five years to financially recover these points and closing costs.

MONTHLY PAYMENTS

In the table below, notice the difference in the monthly payment amounts when the interest rate is at 7%, 8.5%, or 10.0%:

Adjustable rate mortgage payments can be adjusted on a yearly cycle as mentioned earlier. Although you may begin your loan with a low 6%, the adjustment the second year may be as high as two percentage points, up to 8%. On the other hand, the rate could drop to 5.5% or stay the same. It will depend entirely on the economy of the time.

Fixed rate is just that, fixed for the term of the mortgage loan.

The only figure that can change is the escrow amount. This depends on your local taxes and changes in your insurance coverage to keep pace with the growing replacement value of your home.

AMORTIZING A LOAN

Whenever you borrow money, a payment plan is set up to allow you to pay off the loan over a set number

MONTHLY PAYMENT COMPARISONS			
Loan amount	Fixed interest rate	No. of years	Monthly payment
$50,000	7.0%	15	$449.42
$50,000	7.0%	30	$332.66
$50,000	8.5%	15	$492.38
$50,000	8.5%	30	$384.46
$50,000	10.0%	15	$537.31
$50,000	10.0%	30	$438.79

of months. The lender charges you interest on the borrowed money. The total monthly payment includes the principal and interest amount that you will pay during the term of a fixed rate mortgage loan. Keep in mind that the longer the term of your loan and the lower the interest rate, the lower the payments. On the other hand, the shorter the term with the same low interest rates, the higher the payments. What is the real difference to you? Shorter payments will generally save you money that you would otherwise pay in interest over the longer term.

Your lender can provide you with an amortization table for your loan. It will show you how the loan is paid off with each payment; some portion of the payment will go to the principal, and the rest will be paid as interest due on the remaining principal. During the early years of your mortgage, most of the payment is the interest due on the full principal. As the principal decreases, less of your payment is interest and more will go toward the remaining principal. Eventually, the payment will be mostly applied to the remaining principal. During the time you are paying interest on your loan, the total amount of interest paid can be deducted on your income tax at the end of each year that you own the house. Look at the Sample Amortization Schedule for a $20,000 loan at 10% for 96 months:

This table shows a typical small loan, maybe an equity loan on your house. It shows you how the interest and principal amounts are applied throughout the term of the loan.

TYPES OF MORTGAGES TO CONSIDER

A mortgage is a "security instrument" that describes the property as found in the deed and secures the lender for the repayment of the debt evidenced by the note. The two major types of mortgage are conventional loans (usually thirty year or fifteen year) and adjustable rate mortgages (ARMs). There are advantages and disadvantages to both. Other types of financing exist, and you should explore those with your lender if you like. Since most home buyers will opt for one of these two types of loans, they are discussed in more detail below. Veterans Administration loans and Federal Housing Administration loans are also discussed.

SAMPLE AMORTIZATION SCHEDULE

Payment	Month/Year	Payment	Interest	Principal	Balance
					$20,000.00
#1	9/91	$303.49	166.67	136.82	$19,863.18
#2	10/91	$303.49	165.53	137.96	$19,725.22
#3	11/91	$303.49	164.38	139.11	$19,586.11
#4	12/91	$303.49	163.22	140.27	$19,445.84
#49	9/95	$303.49	99.71	203.78	$11,761.63
#93	5/99	$303.49	9.90	293.59	$894.56
#94	6/99	$303.49	7.45	296.04	$598.52
#95	7/99	$303.49	4.99	298.50	$300.02
#96	8/99	$303.49	2.50	300.02	$0.0

Conventional Loan

The thirty-year fixed rate loan is the most common type of mortgage loan. The interest rate never changes with this type of loan, nor does the base amount of the loan. As mentioned above, a 5 to 10% down payment is usually required. The disadvantage to this type of loan is that if the interest rate goes down, the rate on your loan will stay the same. The only way to reduce your interest rate would be to refinance your loan.

A conventional loan is not guaranteed by a government source like the Veterans Administration (VA) or the Federal Housing Administration (FHA), but is secured by the mortgage and a private mortgage insurer. Loans are considered conventional when the payment of the debt rests solely on the ability of the borrower to pay. The ratio of the debt to the value of the property is usually regulated by strict state laws. In other words, the lender will not exceed 75 to 80% of the appraised value of the property in the loan. These loans must be guaranteed by private mortgage insurance (PMI) with the lender named beneficiary.

FHA-Insured Loan

The Federal Housing Administration (FHA) was created in 1934 under the National Housing Act to help provide affordable housing. FHA-insured loans require a small down payment and closing costs from the buyer. Currently, the down payment is calculated at 3% of the first $25,000 and 5% of the balance. The FHA, which operates under the Department of Housing and Urban Development (HUD), only insures a loan on real property made by approved lenders. It does not insure the *property*, but does insure the lender against loss.

VA Mortgage

A veteran who has served a minimum of 180 days of active service since September 16, 1940 (ninety days for veterans of the Korean War) is eligible to apply for a Veterans Administration mortgage. Rules and regulations are issued from time to time by the Veterans Administration, setting forth the qualifications, limitations, and conditions under which a loan may be guaranteed. There is no limitation of the amount of the loan a veteran can obtain; that is determined by the lender. However, the VA usually will set a limit of about 60% of the loan that it will guarantee. In order to determine the proportion of the mortgage loan the VA will guarantee, the veteran must make an application for a certificate of eligibility. The certificate will set forth the amount of benefit (guarantee) to which the veteran is entitled. There is no down payment needed on a VA mortgage, and all closing costs must be paid by the seller. VA loans can be assumed by purchasers who do not qualify as veterans. Veterans Administration Pamphlet 26-4 describes other types of service qualifications for a VA loan guarantee. Write or call:

Veterans Administration
Dept. of Veterans Affairs
Loan Guarantee Service
VA Building
810 Vermont Avenue, N.W.
Washington, DC 20420
(202) 233-2332

Adjustable Rate Mortgage

The Adjustable Rate Mortgage (ARM) offers an interest rate that adjusts up or down within a predetermined "cap" during the entire life of the mortgage. ARMs are based on a lower initial interest rate, which can then change over the life of the loan. Most ARMs have "caps," meaning that there is a limit to the amount the interest rate can fluctuate both annually and over the lifetime of the loan. The best ARMs will have a conversion feature, allowing you to convert the ARM at a low interest rate to a conventional fixed rate loan. There is a fee to convert the loan, and the conversion cannot be done before a certain time period has passed (specific to the particular loan).

Be wary when shopping for an adjustable rate mortgage. Some ARMs have a very low rate to begin with, but you may find your payments have skyrocketed before a year or two is out. Get all the details from your lender and be sure you understand them before you commit to any loan.

Other Types

Apart from the standard mortgages, some creative financing can be done. These arrangements usually depend on the lender and seller. If all parties agree to the arrangement, it may be possible to put together one of many options such as a purchase money mortgage, term loan, amortizing loan, assumable loan, buy-down, balloon payment, blanket mortgage, or rent with option to buy package. Be cautious. Be sure that you understand the conditions of any loan that you get.

Ask the lender about these different types of mortgages and loans if you are interested. Many of them are low-interest guaranteed mortgages. Check around for the best options.

When it comes to financing, people can be very creative.

TIPS TO CONSIDER ABOUT THE LENDER

Review the list below for tips in selecting a source of financing.

1. Ask your Realtor or lawyer about his or her reputation in the mortgage lending market.
2. Compare mortgage rates and terms available with those of other lenders.
3. Determine application fees and other costs.
4. Determine conditions of the mortgage. Is it assumable?
5. Find out the quality of service.
6. Discover types of incentive and low interest, government-guaranteed loans available.
7. Determine attitudes toward single buyers.

Try not to feel intimidated when first talking with the loan officer. He or she should be friendly and able to guide you through this experience. Ask questions and jot down notes. Bring a friend along with you to help you remember important points and to keep you from being too nervous.

THE APPOINTMENT

At the appointment to apply for the loan, the loan officer will expect you to have accurate information for the interview. It is wise to bring the following information with you:

- The signed Agreement of Sale or a copy of it.
- A copy of your income tax returns for two to five years. Be prepared for a difficult review if you are self-employed.
- A recent pay stub from your employer and/or a letter of employment verification.
- A list of your current assets (available money in checking and savings accounts, stocks, bonds, notes receivable, interest earnings, automobile, other sources of income).
- A list of your current liabilities (debts, loans, credit card payments, car payments, lease obligations).

The bank will determine your net worth. You can determine your net worth on your own by completing the Personal Net Worth form below.

NET WORTH

Assets	(minus)	Liabilities	=	Net Worth
$125,000		$ 65,000	=	$ 60,000

The loan officer will use this information to determine whether you qualify for the mortgage obligation you are requesting. The loan officer will conduct the interview, gather the information, and take the application fee at this time. You will be told that the processing takes three to four weeks for loan approval. Unless there is an unexpected finding in your credit or debt history, you will receive your mortgage confirmation notice with a Truth in Lending Form for your signature in the mail within a month or so.

When you receive the Loan Commitment notification from the Lender, you will have to notify the Realtor or your Lawyer. Once you have been approved for your loan, a settlement date will be set with the seller, the lender, and the buyer by the Realtor or your lawyer.

TAXES, YOUR HOME, AND YOU

Just what does it mean to you to own a house when tax time comes around? It means that you pay real estate taxes and possibly school taxes on the house you bought either as escrow or when billed by the local government.

It means that on a $100,000 home about $2,000 needs to be budgeted to cover taxes, which is usually through escrow. What do you get to deduct from income taxes when you own a home? Only the interest payments on your mortgage are tax deductible until you sell the property or if you rent it. If you sell or rent the property, the costs you have had or continue to have to maintain it or improve it can sometimes be deducted from your tax burden. Your accountant will assist you with this issue. Usually, the improvements you make to a house while you live in it help it to increase in value. At the same time, the costs of those improvements will be calculated into your deductions in the year that you sell the property, not as deductions each tax year. This is a very tricky area, and you should consult your tax accountant and/or attorney.

QUICK CHECKLIST
FINANCING

1. Have you shopped around to at least three lenders to compare fees, rates, and services?
2. Have you worked out your net worth ahead of time?
3. Do you know what type of mortgage you want?
4. Do you know what type of financing is available to you?
5. Have you established a strong credit history?
6. Do you have a stable employment history?
7. Do you feel confident about meeting with the loan officer?
8. Do you know what you can afford?
9. Do you know that you will have three business days to cancel the transaction with the lender? Be sure that you understand possible costs.
10. Have you checked on escrow costs?
11. Are you prepared for your mortgage loan appointment meeting? Take documents that you will need to the meeting.

MORTGAGE

THIS MORTGAGE ("Security Instrument") is given on .... The mortgagor is ....
....
("Borrower"). This Security Instrument is given to ....
....
.... , which is organized and existing under the laws of ....
.... , and whose address is ....
....
("Lender"). Borrower owes Lender the principal sum of ....
.... Dollars (U.S. $...). This debt is evidenced by Borrower's note dated the same date as this Security Instrument ("Note"), which provides for monthly payments, with the full debt, if not paid earlier, due and payable on .... This Security Instrument secures to Lender: (a) the repayment of the debt evidenced by the Note, with interest, and all renewals, extensions and modifications of the Note; (b) the payment of all other sums, with interest, advanced under paragraph 7 to protect the security of this Security Instrument; and (c) the performance of Borrower's covenants and agreements under this Security Instrument and the Note. For this purpose, Borrower does hereby mortgage, grant and convey to Lender the following described property located in .... County, Pennsylvania:

which has the address of .... , ... ,
                                                    [Street]   [City]

Pennsylvania .... ("Property Address");
                    [Zip Code]

PENNSYLVANIA—Single Family—Fannie Mae/Freddie Mac UNIFORM INSTRUMENT   Form 3039 9/90 *(page 1 of 6 pages)*

BANKERS SYSTEMS, INC., ST. CLOUD, MN 56302 (1-800-397-2341) FORM MD-1-PA 2/13/91   _____   _____

TOGETHER WITH all the improvements now or hereafter erected on the property, and all easements, appurtenances, and fixtures now or hereafter a part of the property. All replacements and additions shall also be covered by this Security Instrument. All of the foregoing is referred to in this Security Instrument as the "Property."

BORROWER COVENANTS that Borrower is lawfully seised of the estate hereby conveyed and has the right to mortgage, grant and convey the Property and that the Property is unencumbered, except for encumbrances of record. Borrower warrants and will defend generally the title to the Property against all claims and demands, subject to any encumbrances of record.

THIS SECURITY INSTRUMENT combines uniform covenants for national use and non-uniform covenants with limited variations by jurisdiction to constitute a uniform security instrument covering real property.

UNIFORM COVENANTS. Borrower and Lender covenant and agree as follows:

1. Payment of Principal and Interest; Prepayment and Late Charges. Borrower shall promptly pay when due the principal of and interest on the debt evidenced by the Note and any prepayment and late charges due under the Note.

2. Funds for Taxes and Insurance. Subject to applicable law or to a written waiver by Lender, Borrower shall pay to Lender on the day monthly payments are due under the Note, until the Note is paid in full, a sum ("Funds") for: (a) yearly taxes and assessments which may attain priority over this Security Instrument as a lien on the Property; (b) yearly leasehold payments or ground rents on the Property, if any; (c) yearly hazard or property insurance premiums; (d) yearly flood insurance premiums, if any; (e) yearly mortgage insurance premiums, if any; and (f) any sums payable by Borrower to Lender, in accordance with the provisions of paragraph 8, in lieu of the payment of mortgage insurance premiums. These items are called "Escrow Items." Lender may, at any time, collect and hold Funds in an amount not to exceed the maximum amount a lender for a federally related mortgage loan may require for Borrower's escrow account under the federal Real Estate Settlement Procedures Act of 1974 as amended from time to time, 12 U.S.C. § 2601 *et seq.* ("RESPA"), unless another law that applies to the Funds sets a lesser amount. If so, Lender may, at any time, collect and hold Funds in an amount not to exceed the lesser amount. Lender may estimate the amount of Funds due on the basis of current data and reasonable estimates of expenditures of future Escrow Items or otherwise in accordance with applicable law.

The Funds shall be held in an institution whose deposits are insured by a federal agency, instrumentality, or entity (including Lender, if Lender is such an institution) or in any Federal Home Loan Bank. Lender shall apply the Funds to pay the Escrow Items. Lender may not charge Borrower for holding and applying the Funds, annually analyzing the escrow account, or verifying the Escrow Items, unless Lender pays Borrower interest on the Funds and applicable law permits Lender to make such a charge. However, Lender may require Borrower to pay a one-time charge for an independent real estate tax reporting service used by Lender in connection with this loan, unless applicable law provides otherwise. Unless an agreement is made or applicable law requires interest to be paid, Lender shall not be required to pay Borrower any interest or earnings on the Funds. Borrower and Lender may agree in writing, however, that interest shall be paid on the Funds. Lender shall give to Borrower, without charge, an annual accounting of the Funds, showing credits and debits to the Funds and the purpose for which each debit to the Funds was made. The Funds are pledged as additional security for all sums secured by this Security Instrument.

If the Funds held by Lender exceed the amounts permitted to be held by applicable law, Lender shall account to Borrower for the excess Funds in accordance with the requirements of applicable law. If the amount of the Funds held by Lender at any time is not sufficient to pay the Escrow Items when due, Lender may so notify Borrower in writing, and, in such case Borrower shall pay to Lender the amount necessary to make up the deficiency. Borrower shall make up the deficiency in no more than twelve monthly payments, at Lender's sole discretion.

Upon payment in full of all sums secured by this Security Instrument, Lender shall promptly refund to Borrower any Funds held by Lender. If, under paragraph 21, Lender shall acquire or sell the Property, Lender, prior to the acquisition or sale of the Property, shall apply any Funds held by Lender at the time of acquisition or sale as a credit against the sums secured by this Security Instrument.

3. Application of Payments. Unless applicable law provides otherwise, all payments received by Lender under paragraphs 1 and 2 shall be applied: first, to any prepayment charges due under the Note; second, to amounts payable under paragraph 2; third, to interest due; fourth, to principal due; and last, to any late charges due under the Note.

4. Charges; Liens. Borrower shall pay all taxes, assessments, charges, fines and impositions attributable to the Property which may attain priority over this Security Instrument, and leasehold payments or ground rents, if any. Borrower shall pay these obligations in the manner provided in paragraph 2, or if not paid in that manner, Borrower shall pay them on time directly to the person owed payment. Borrower shall promptly furnish to Lender all notices of amounts to be paid under this paragraph. If Borrower makes these payments directly, Borrower shall promptly furnish to Lender receipts evidencing the payments.

Borrower shall promptly discharge any lien which has priority over this Security Instrument unless Borrower: (a) agrees in writing to the payment of the obligation secured by the lien in a manner acceptable to Lender; (b) contests in good faith the lien by, or defends against enforcement of the lien in, legal proceedings which in the Lender's opinion operate to prevent the enforcement of the lien; or (c) secures from the holder of the lien an agreement satisfactory to Lender subordinating the lien to this Security Instrument. If Lender determines that any part of the Property is subject to a lien which may attain priority over this Security Instrument, Lender may give Borrower a notice identifying the lien. Borrower shall satisfy the lien or take one or more of the actions set forth above within 10 days of the giving of notice.

Form 3039 9/90 *(page 2 of 6 pages)*

5. Hazard or Property Insurance. Borrower shall keep the improvements now existing or hereafter erected on the Property insured against loss by fire, hazards included within the term "extended coverage" and any other hazards, including floods or flooding, for which Lender requires insurance. This insurance shall be maintained in the amounts and for the periods that Lender requires. The insurance carrier providing the insurance shall be chosen by Borrower subject to Lender's approval which shall not be unreasonably withheld. If Borrower fails to maintain coverage described above, Lender may, at Lender's option, obtain coverage to protect Lender's rights in the Property in accordance with paragraph 7.

All insurance policies and renewals shall be acceptable to Lender and shall include a standard mortgage clause. Lender shall have the right to hold the policies and renewals. If Lender requires, Borrower shall promptly give to Lender all receipts of paid premiums and renewal notices. In the event of loss, Borrower shall give prompt notice to the insurance carrier and Lender. Lender may make proof of loss if not made promptly by Borrower.

Unless Lender and Borrower otherwise agree in writing, insurance proceeds shall be applied to restoration or repair of the Property damaged, if the restoration or repair is economically feasible and Lender's security is not lessened. If the restoration or repair is not economically feasible or Lender's security would be lessened, the insurance proceeds shall be applied to the sums secured by this Security Instrument, whether or not then due, with any excess paid to Borrower. If Borrower abandons the Property, or does not answer within 30 days a notice from Lender that the insurance carrier has offered to settle a claim, then Lender may collect the insurance proceeds. Lender may use the proceeds to repair or restore the Property or to pay sums secured by this Security Instrument, whether or not then due. The 30-day period will begin when the notice is given.

Unless Lender and Borrower otherwise agree in writing, any application of proceeds to principal shall not extend or postpone the due date of the monthly payments referred to in paragraphs 1 and 2 or change the amount of the payments. If under paragraph 21 the Property is acquired by Lender, Borrower's right to any insurance policies and proceeds resulting from damage to the Property prior to the acquisition shall pass to Lender to the extent of the sums secured by this Security Instrument immediately prior to the acquisition.

6. Occupancy, Preservation, Maintenance and Protection of the Property; Borrower's Loan Application; Leaseholds. Borrower shall occupy, establish, and use the Property as Borrower's principal residence within sixty days after the execution of this Security Instrument and shall continue to occupy the Property as Borrower's principal residence for at least one year after the date of occupancy, unless Lender otherwise agrees in writing, which consent shall not be unreasonably withheld, or unless extenuating circumstances exist which are beyond Borrower's control. Borrower shall not destroy, damage or impair the Property, allow the Property to deteriorate, or commit waste on the Property. Borrower shall be in default if any forfeiture action or proceeding, whether civil or criminal, is begun that in Lender's good faith judgment could result in forfeiture of the Property or otherwise materially impair the lien created by this Security Instrument or Lender's security interest. Borrower may cure such a default and reinstate, as provided in paragraph 18, by causing the action or proceeding to be dismissed with a ruling that, in Lender's good faith determination, precludes forfeiture of the Borrower's interest in the Property or other material impairment of the lien created by this Security Instrument or Lender's security interest. Borrower shall also be in default if Borrower, during the loan application process, gave materially false or inaccurate information or statements to Lender (or failed to provide Lender with any material information) in connection with the loan evidenced by the Note, including, but not limited to, representations concerning Borrower's occupancy of the Property as a principal residence. If this Security Instrument is on a leasehold, Borrower shall comply with all the provisions of the lease. If Borrower acquires fee title to the Property, the leasehold and the fee title shall not merge unless Lender agrees to the merger in writing.

7. Protection of Lender's Rights in the Property. If Borrower fails to perform the covenants and agreements contained in this Security Instrument, or there is a legal proceeding that may significantly affect Lender's rights in the Property (such as a proceeding in bankruptcy, probate, for condemnation or forfeiture or to enforce laws or regulations), then Lender may do and pay for whatever is necessary to protect the value of the Property and Lender's rights in the Property. Lender's actions may include paying any sums secured by a lien which has priority over this Security Instrument, appearing in court, paying reasonable attorneys' fees and entering on the Property to make repairs. Although Lender may take action under this paragraph 7, Lender does not have to do so.

Any amounts disbursed by Lender under this paragraph 7 shall become additional debt of Borrower secured by this Security Instrument. Unless Borrower and Lender agree to other terms of payment, these amounts shall bear interest from the date of disbursement at the Note rate and shall be payable, with interest, upon notice from Lender to Borrower requesting payment.

8. Mortgage Insurance. If Lender required mortgage insurance as a condition of making the loan secured by this Security Instrument, Borrower shall pay the premiums required to maintain the mortgage insurance in effect. If, for any reason, the mortgage insurance coverage required by Lender lapses or ceases to be in effect, Borrower shall pay the premiums required to obtain coverage substantially equivalent to the mortgage insurance previously in effect, at a cost substantially equivalent to the cost to Borrower of the mortgage insurance previously in effect, from an alternate mortgage insurer approved by Lender. If substantially equivalent mortgage insurance coverage is not available, Borrower shall pay to Lender each month a sum equal to one-twelfth of the yearly mortgage insurance premium being paid by Borrower when the insurance coverage lapsed or ceased to be in effect. Lender will accept, use and retain these payments as a loss reserve in lieu of mortgage insurance. Loss reserve payments may no longer be required, at the option of Lender, if mortgage insurance

Form 3039 9/90 *(page 3 of 6 pages)*

coverage (in the amount and for the period that Lender requires) provided by an insurer approved by Lender again becomes available and is obtained. Borrower shall pay the premiums required to maintain mortgage insurance in effect, or to provide a loss reserve, until the requirement for mortgage insurance ends in accordance with any written agreement between Borrower and Lender or applicable law.

9. Inspection. Lender or its agent may make reasonable entries upon and inspections of the Property. Lender shall give Borrower notice at the time of or prior to an inspection specifying reasonable cause for the inspection.

10. Condemnation. The proceeds of any award or claim for damages, direct or consequential, in connection with any condemnation or other taking of any part of the Property, or for conveyance in lieu of condemnation, are hereby assigned and shall be paid to Lender.

In the event of a total taking of the Property, the proceeds shall be applied to the sums secured by this Security Instrument, whether or not then due, with any excess paid to Borrower. In the event of a partial taking of the Property in which the fair market value of the Property immediately before the taking is equal to or greater than the amount of the sums secured by this Security Instrument immediately before the taking, unless Borrower and Lender otherwise agree in writing, the sums secured by this Security Instrument shall be reduced by the amount of the proceeds multiplied by the following fraction: (a) the total amount of the sums secured immediately before the taking, divided by (b) the fair market value of the Property immediately before the taking. Any balance shall be paid to Borrower. In the event of a partial taking of the Property in which the fair market value of the Property immediately before the taking is less than the amount of the sums secured immediately before the taking, unless Borrower and Lender otherwise agree in writing or unless applicable law otherwise provides, the proceeds shall be applied to the sums secured by this Security Instrument whether or not the sums are then due.

If the Property is abandoned by Borrower, or if, after notice by Lender to Borrower that the condemnor offers to make an award or settle a claim for damages, Borrower fails to respond to Lender within 30 days after the date the notice is given, Lender is authorized to collect and apply the proceeds, at its option, either to restoration or repair of the Property or to the sums secured by this Security Instrument, whether or not then due.

Unless Lender and Borrower otherwise agree in writing, any application of proceeds to principal shall not extend or postpone the due date of the monthly payments referred to in paragraphs 1 and 2 or change the amount of such payments.

11. Borrower Not Released; Forbearance By Lender Not a Waiver. Extension of the time for payment or modification of amortization of the sums secured by this Security Instrument granted by Lender to any successor in interest of Borrower shall not operate to release the liability of the original Borrower or Borrower's successors in interest. Lender shall not be required to commence proceedings against any successor in interest or refuse to extend time for payment or otherwise modify amortization of the sums secured by this Security Instrument by reason of any demand made by the original Borrower or Borrower's successors in interest. Any forbearance by Lender in exercising any right or remedy shall not be a waiver of or preclude the exercise of any right or remedy.

12. Successors and Assigns Bound; Joint and Several Liability; Co-signers. The covenants and agreements of this Security Instrument shall bind and benefit the successors and assigns of Lender and Borrower, subject to the provisions of paragraph 17. Borrower's covenants and agreements shall be joint and several. Any Borrower who co-signs this Security Instrument but does not execute the Note: (a) is co-signing this Security Instrument only to mortgage, grant and convey that Borrower's interest in the Property under the terms of this Security Instrument; (b) is not personally obligated to pay the sums secured by this Security Instrument; and (c) agrees that Lender and any other Borrower may agree to extend, modify, forbear or make any accommodations with regard to the terms of this Security Instrument or the Note without that Borrower's consent.

13. Application of Payments. If the loan secured by this Security Instrument is subject to a law which sets maximum loan charges, and that law is finally interpreted so that the interest or other loan charges collected or to be collected in connection with the loan exceed the permitted limits, then: (a) any such loan charge shall be reduced by the amount necessary to reduce the charge to the permitted limit; and (b) any sums already collected from Borrower which exceeded permitted limits will be refunded to Borrower. Lender may choose to make this refund by reducing the principal owed under the Note or by making a direct payment to Borrower. If a refund reduces principal, the reduction will be treated as a partial prepayment without any prepayment charge under the Note.

14. Notices. Any notice to Borrower provided for in this Security Instrument shall be given by delivering it or by mailing it by first class mail unless applicable law requires use of another method. The notice shall be directed to the Property Address or any other address Borrower designates by notice to Lender. Any notice to Lender shall be given by first class mail to Lender's address stated herein or any other address Lender designates by notice to Borrower. Any notice provided for in this Security Instrument shall be deemed to have been given to Borrower or Lender when given as provided in this paragraph.

15. Governing Law; Severability. This Security Instrument shall be governed by federal law and the law of the jurisdiction in which the Property is located. In the event that any provision or clause of this Security Instrument or the Note conflicts with applicable law, such conflict shall not affect other provisions of this Security Instrument or the Note which can be given effect without the conflicting provision. To this end the provisions of this Security Instrument and the Note are declared to be severable.

Form 3039 9/90 *(page 4 of 6 pages)*

16. Borrower's Copy. Borrower shall be given one conformed copy of the Note and of this Security Instrument.

17. Transfer of the Property or a Beneficial Interest in Borrower. If all or any part of the Property or any interest in it is sold or transferred (or if a beneficial interest in Borrower is sold or transferred and Borrower is not a natural person) without Lender's prior written consent, Lender may, at its option, require immediate payment in full of all sums secured by this Security Instrument. However, this option shall not be exercised by Lender if exercise is prohibited by federal law as of the date of this Security Instrument.

If Lender exercises this option, Lender shall give Borrower notice of acceleration. The notice shall provide a period of not less than 30 days from the date the notice is delivered or mailed within which Borrower must pay all sums secured by this Security Instrument. If Borrower fails to pay these sums prior to the expiration of this period, Lender may invoke any remedies permitted by this Security Instrument without further notice or demand on Borrower.

18. Borrower's Right to Reinstate. If Borrower meets certain conditions, Borrower shall have the right to have enforcement of this Security Instrument discontinued at any time prior to the earlier of: (a) 5 days (or such other period as applicable law may specify for reinstatement) before sale of the Property pursuant to any power of sale contained in this Security Instrument; or (b) entry of a judgment enforcing this Security Instrument. Those conditions are that Borrower: (a) pays Lender all sums which then would be due under this Security Instrument and the Note as if no acceleration had occurred; (b) cures any default of any other covenants or agreements; (c) pays all expenses incurred in enforcing this Security Instrument, including, but not limited to, reasonable attorneys' fees; and (d) takes such action as Lender may reasonably require to assure that the lien of this Security Instrument, Lender's rights in the Property and Borrower's obligation to pay the sums secured by this Security Instrument shall continue unchanged. Upon reinstatement by Borrower, this Security Instrument and the obligations secured hereby shall remain fully effective as if no acceleration had occurred. However, this right to reinstate shall not apply in the case of acceleration under paragraph 17.

19. Sale of Note; Change of Loan Servicer. The Note or a partial interest in the Note (together with this Security Instrument) may be sold one or more times without prior notice to Borrower. A sale may result in a change in the entity (known as the "Loan Servicer") that collects monthly payments due under the Note and this Security Instrument. There also may be one or more changes of the Loan Servicer unrelated to a sale of the Note. If there is a change of the Loan Servicer, Borrower will be given written notice of the change in accordance with paragraph 14 above and applicable law. The notice will state the name and address of the new Loan Servicer and the address to which payments should be made. The notice will also contain any other information required by applicable law.

20. Hazardous Substances. Borrower shall not cause or permit the presence, use, disposal, storage, or release of any Hazardous Substances on or in the Property. Borrower shall not do, nor allow anyone else to do, anything affecting the Property that is in violation of any Environmental Law. The preceding two sentences shall not apply to the presence, use, or storage on the Property of small quantities of Hazardous Substances that are generally recognized to be appropriate to normal residential uses and to maintenance of the Property.

Borrower shall promptly give Lender written notice of any investigation, claim, demand, lawsuit or other action by any governmental or regulatory agency or private party involving the Property and any Hazardous Substance or Environmental Law of which Borrower has actual knowledge. If Borrower learns, or is notified by any governmental or regulatory authority, that any removal or other remediation of any Hazardous Substance affecting the Property is necessary, Borrower shall promptly take all necessary remedial actions in accordance with Environmental Law.

As used in this paragraph 20, "Hazardous Substances" are those substances defined as toxic or hazardous substances by Environmental Law and the following substances: gasoline, kerosene, other flammable or toxic petroleum products, toxic pesticides and herbicides, volatile solvents, materials containing asbestos or formaldehyde, and radioactive materials. As used in this paragraph 20, "Environmental Law" means federal laws and laws of the jurisdiction where the Property is located that relate to health, safety or environmental protection.

NON-UNIFORM COVENANTS. Borrower and Lender further covenant and agree as follows:

21. Acceleration; Remedies. Lender shall give notice to Borrower prior to acceleration following Borrower's breach of any covenant or agreement in this Security Instrument (but not prior to acceleration under paragraph 17 unless applicable law provides otherwise). Lender shall notify Borrower of, among other things: (a) the default; (b) the action required to cure the default; (c) when the default must be cured; and (d) that failure to cure the default as specified may result in acceleration of the sums secured by this Security Instrument, foreclosure by judicial proceeding and sale of the Property. Lender shall further inform Borrower of the right to reinstate after acceleration and the right to assert in the foreclosure proceeding the non-existence of a default or any other defense of Borrower to acceleration and foreclosure. If the default is not cured as specified, Lender at its option may require immediate payment in full of all sums secured by this Security Instrument without further demand and may foreclose this Security Instrument by judicial proceeding. Lender shall be entitled to collect all expenses incurred in pursuing the remedies provided in this paragraph 21, including, but not limited to, attorneys' fees and costs of title evidence to the extent permitted by applicable law.

22. Release. Upon payment of all sums secured by this Security Instrument, this Security Instrument and the estate conveyed shall terminate and become void. After such occurrence, Lender shall discharge and satisfy this Security Instrument without charge to Borrower. Borrower shall pay any recordation costs.

Form 3039 9/90 *(page 5 of 6 pages)*

BANKERS SYSTEMS, INC., ST. CLOUD, MN 56302 (1-800-397-2341) FORM MD-1-PA 2/13/91

23. Waivers. Borrower, to the extent permitted by applicable law, waives and releases any error or defects in proceedings to enforce this Security Instrument, and hereby waives the benefit of any present or future laws providing for stay of execution, extension of time, exemption from attachment, levy and sale, and homestead exemption.

24. Reinstatement Period. Borrower's time to reinstate provided in paragraph 18 shall extend to one hour prior to the commencement of bidding at a sheriff's sale or other sale pursuant to this Security Instrument.

25. Purchase Money Mortgage. If any of the debt secured by this Security Instrument is lent to Borrower to acquire title to the Property, this Security Instrument shall be a purchase money mortgage.

26. Interest Rate After Judgment. Borrower agrees that the interest rate payable after a judgment is entered on the Note or in an action of mortgage foreclosure shall be the rate payable from time to time under the Note.

27. Riders to this Security Instrument. If one or more riders are executed by Borrower and recorded together with this Security Instrument, the covenants and agreements of each such rider shall be incorporated into and shall amend and supplement the covenants and agreements of this Security Instrument as if the rider(s) were a part of this Security Instrument. [Check applicable box(es)]

☐ Adjustable Rate Rider   ☐ Condominium Rider   ☐ 1–4 Family Rider
☐ Graduated Payment Rider   ☐ Planned Unit Development Rider   ☐ Biweekly Payment Rider
☐ Balloon Rider   ☐ Rate Improvement Rider   ☐ Second Home Rider
☐ Other(s) [specify]

BY SIGNING BELOW, Borrower accepts and agrees to the terms and covenants contained in this Security Instrument and in any rider(s) executed by Borrower and recorded with it.

Witnesses:

.... (Seal)
                                                                                                    –Borrower

                                                         Social Security Number ....

.... (Seal)
                                                                                                    –Borrower

                                                         Social Security Number ....

———————————— **[Space Below This Line For Acknowledgment]** ————————————

COMMONWEALTH OF PENNSYLVANIA, ... County ss:

On this, the .... day of .... , before me, ...
.... the undersigned officer, personally appeared...
.... known to me (or satisfactorily proven) to be the person .... whose name .... subscribed to the within instrument and acknowledged that .... executed the same for the purposes herein contained.

IN WITNESS WHEREOF, I hereunto set my hand and official seal.

My Commission expires:

                                            ....

                                            ....
                                                            Title of Officer

ADJUSTABLE RATE RIDER

THIS ADJUSTABLE RATE RIDER is made this .... day of ....
and is incorporated into and shall be deemed to amend and supplement the Mortgage, Deed of Trust or Security
Deed (the "Security Instrument") of the same date given by the undersigned (the "Borrower") to secure Borrower's
Adjustable Rate Note (the "Note") to ....
.... (the "Lender")
of the same date and covering the property described in the Security Instrument and located at:

....
[Property Address]

NOTICE: THE SECURITY INSTRUMENT SECURES A NOTE WHICH CONTAINS A PROVISION ALLOWING FOR CHANGES IN THE INTEREST RATE. INCREASES IN THE INTEREST RATE WILL RESULT IN HIGHER PAYMENTS. DECREASES IN THE INTEREST RATE WILL RESULT IN LOWER PAYMENTS.

ADDITIONAL COVENANTS. In addition to the covenants and agreements made in the Security Instrument, Borrower and Lender further covenant and agree as follows:

A. INTEREST RATE AND SCHEDULED PAYMENT CHANGES

The Note provides for an initial interest rate of .... %. The Note provides for changes in the interest rate and the payments, as follows:

3. PAYMENTS

(A) Scheduled Payments

All references in the Security Instrument to "monthly payments" are changed to "scheduled payments."
I will pay principal and interest by making payments when scheduled: (mark one):
☐ I will make my scheduled payments on the first day of each month beginning on ....
....
☐ I will make my scheduled payments as follows:

☐ In addition to the payments described above, I will pay a "balloon payment" of $ ....
on .... The Note Holder will deliver or mail to me notice prior to
maturity that the balloon payment is due. This notice will state the balloon payment amount and the date that it is due.

(B) Maturity Date and Place of Payments

I will make these payments as scheduled until I have paid all of the principal and interest and any other charges described in the Note.
My scheduled payments will be applied to interest before principal. If, on ....
.... , I still owe amounts under the Note, I will pay those amounts in full on that date, which is called the "maturity date."
I will make my scheduled payments at ....
.... or at a different place if required by the Note Holder.

(C) Amount of My Initial Scheduled Payments

Each of my initial scheduled payments will be in the amount of U.S. $ .... This amount may change.

(D) Scheduled Payment Changes

Changes in my scheduled payment will reflect changes in the unpaid principal of my loan and in the interest rate that I must pay. The Note Holder will determine my new interest rate and the changed amount of my scheduled payment in accordance with Section 4 of the Note.

4. INTEREST RATE AND SCHEDULED PAYMENT CHANGES

(A) Change Dates

Each date on which my interest rate could change is called a "Change Date." (Mark one)

☐ The interest rate I will pay may change on the first day of .... and on that day every .... month thereafter.

☐ The interest rate I will pay may change .... and on every .... thereafter.

(B) The Index

Beginning with the first Change Date, my interest rate will be based on an Index. The "Index" is: ....
....
....
....

The most recent Index figure available as of the date ☐ 45 days   ☐ .... before each Change Date is called the "Current Index."

If the Index is no longer available, the Note Holder will choose a new index which is based upon comparable information. The Note Holder will give me notice of this choice.

(C) Calculation of Changes

Before each Change Date, the Note Holder will calculate my new interest rate by ....
.... percentage points (........................... %) to the Current Index. The result of this calculation:

☐ will not be rounded off.

☐ will be rounded off by the Note Holder to the nearest _____ %.

☐ will be rounded off by the Note Holder up to the nearest _____ %.

☐ will be rounded off by the Note Holder down to the nearest _____ %.

Subject to the limitations stated in Section 4(D) below, this amount will be my new interest rate until the next change date.

The Note Holder will then determine the amount of the scheduled payment that would be sufficient to repay the unpaid principal that I am expected to owe at the Change Date in full on the maturity date at my new interest rate in substantially equal payments. The result of this calculation will be the new amount of my scheduled payment.

(D) Limits on Interest Rate Changes

☐ My interest rate will never be increased or decreased on any single change date by more than ....
    percentage points from the rate of interest I have been paying for the preceding period.

☐ My interest rate will never be greater than ....% or less than ....%.

(E) Effective Date of Changes

My new interest rate will become effective on each Change Date. I will pay the amount of my new scheduled payment beginning on the first scheduled payment date after the Change Date until the amount of my scheduled payment changes again.

(F) Notice of Changes

At least 25 days, but no more than 120 days, before the effective date of any payment change, the Note Holder will deliver or mail to me a notice of any changes in my interest rate and the amount of my scheduled payment. The notice will include information required by law to be given me and also the title and telephone number of a person who will answer any question I may have regarding the notice.

B. FUNDS FOR TAXES AND INSURANCE

[Mark one]

☐ Uniform Covenant 2 of the Security Instrument is waived by the Lender.

☐ Uniform Covenant 2 of the Security Instrument is amended to read as follows:

2. SCHEDULED PAYMENTS FOR TAXES AND INSURANCE

(A) Borrower's Obligations

I will pay to Lender all amounts necessary to pay for taxes, assessments, leasehold payments or ground rents (if any), and hazard insurance on the Property and mortgage insurance (if any). I will pay those amounts to Lender unless Lender tells me, in writing, that I do not have to do so, or unless the law requires otherwise. I will make those payments on the same day that my scheduled payments of principal and interest are due under the Note.

Each of my payments under this Paragraph 2 will be the sum of the following:

    (i) The estimated yearly taxes and assessments on the Property which under the law may be superior to this Security Instrument, divided by the number of scheduled payments in a year; plus,

    (ii) The estimated yearly leasehold payments or ground rents on the Property, if any, divided by the number of scheduled payments in a year; plus

(iii) The estimated yearly premium for hazard insurance covering the Property, divided by the number of scheduled payments in a year; plus

(iv) The estimated yearly premium for mortgage insurance (if any), divided by the number of scheduled payments in a year.

Lender will estimate from time to time my yearly taxes, assessments, leasehold payments or ground rents and insurance premiums, which will be called the "escrow items." Lender will use existing assessments and bills and reasonable estimates of future assessments and bills. The amounts that I pay to Lender for escrow items under this Paragraph 2 will be called the "Funds".

(B) Lender's Obligations

Lender will keep the Funds in a savings or banking institution which has its deposits or accounts insured or guaranteed by a federal or state agency. If Lender is such an institution, Lender may hold the Funds. Except as described in this Paragraph 2, Lender will use the Funds to pay the escrow items. Lender will give to me, without charge, an annual accounting of the Funds. That accounting must show all additions to and deductions from the Funds and the reason for each deduction.

Lender may not charge me for holding or keeping the Funds, for using the Funds to pay escrow items, for analyzing my payments of Funds, or for receiving, verifying and totaling assessments and bills. However, Lender may charge me for these services if Lender pays me interest on the Funds and if the law permits Lender to make such a charge. Lender will not be required to pay me any interest or earnings on the Funds unless either (i) Lender and I agree in writing, at the time I sign this Security Instrument, that Lender will pay interest on the Funds: or (ii) the law requires Lender to pay interest on the Funds.

(C) Adjustments to the Funds

If Lender's estimates are too high or if taxes and insurance rates go down, the amounts that I pay under this Paragraph 2 will be too large. If this happens at a time when I am keeping all of my promises and agreements made in this Security Instrument, I will have the right to have the excess amount either promptly repaid to me as a direct refund or credited to my future scheduled payments of Funds. There will be excess amounts if, at any time, the sum of (i) the amount of Funds which Lender is holding or keeping, plus (ii) the amount of the scheduled payments of Funds which I still must pay between that time and the due dates of escrow items is greater than the amount necessary to pay the escrow items when they are due.

If, when payments of escrow items are due, Lender has not received enough Funds to make those payments, I will pay to Lender whatever additional amount is necessary to pay the escrow items in full. I must pay that additional amount in one or more payments as Lender may require.

When I have paid all of the sums secured, Lender will promptly refund to me any Funds that are then being held by Lender. If, as a result of the exercise by Lender of any of its rights under this Security Instrument, either Lender acquires the Property or the Property is sold, then immediately before the acquisition or sale, Lender will use any Funds which Lender is holding at the time to reduce the sums secured.

BY SIGNING BELOW, Borrower accepts and agrees to the terms and covenants contained in this Adjustable Rate Rider.

.... (Seal)
                                                      -Borrower

.... (Seal)
                                                      -Borrower

ADJUSTABLE RATE NOTE

NOTICE TO BORROWER: THIS NOTE CONTAINS A PROVISION ALLOWING FOR CHANGES IN THE INTEREST RATE. INCREASES IN THE INTEREST RATE WILL RESULT IN HIGHER PAYMENTS. DECREASES IN THE INTEREST RATE WILL RESULT IN LOWER PAYMENTS.

.... , ... ,
          [Date]   [City]   [State]

....
                                              [Property Address]

1. BORROWER'S PROMISE TO PAY

In return for a loan that I have received, I promise to pay U.S. $.. (this amount is called "principal"), plus interest, to the order of the Lender. The Lender is ....
....
....
I understand that the Lender may transfer this Note. The Lender or anyone who takes this Note by transfer and who is entitled to receive payments under this Note is called the "Note Holder."

2. INTEREST

Interest will be charged on unpaid principal until the full amount of principal has been paid. I will pay interest at a yearly rate of ....%. The interest rate I will pay will change in accordance with Section 4 of this Note.

The interest rate required by this Section 2 and Section 4 of this Note is the rate I will pay both before and after any default described in Section 7(C) of this Note. Interest will be calculated on a ....
basis.

3. PAYMENTS

(A) Scheduled Payments

I will pay principal and interest by making payments when scheduled: (mark one)

☐ I will make my scheduled payments on the first day of each month beginning on ....
☐ I will make scheduled payments as follows:

☐ In addition to the payments described above, I will pay a "balloon payment" of $...
on .... The Note Holder will deliver or mail to me notice prior to maturity that the balloon payment is due. This notice will state the balloon payment amount and the date that it is due.

(B) Maturity Date and Place of Payments

I will make these payments as scheduled until I have paid all of the principal and interest and any other charges described below that I may owe under this Note.

My scheduled payments will be applied to interest before principal. If, on .... ,
I still owe amounts under this Note, I will pay those amounts in full on that date, which is called the "maturity date."

I will make my scheduled payments at ....
.... or at a different place if required by the Note Holder.

(C) Amount of My Initial Scheduled Payments

Each of my initial scheduled payments will be in the amount of U.S. $... This amount may change.

(D) Scheduled Payment Changes

Changes in my scheduled payments will reflect changes in the unpaid principal of my loan and in the interest rate that I must pay. The Note Holder will determine my new interest rate and the changed amount of my scheduled payment in accordance with Section 4 of this Note.

MULTISTATE ADJUSTABLE RATE NOTE –   **Form ADJ-NOTE 5/1/91** *(page 1 of 4)*

4. INTEREST RATE AND SCHEDULED PAYMENT CHANGES

(A) Change Dates

Each date on which my interest rate could change is called a "Change Date." (Mark one)

☐ The interest rate I will pay may change on the first day of .... and on that day every .... month thereafter.

☐ The interest rate I will pay may change .... and on every .... thereafter.

(B) The Index

Beginning with the first Change Date, my interest rate will be based on an Index. The "Index" is: ....

....

....

....

The most recent Index figure available as of the date   ☐ 45 days   ☐ .... before each Change Date is called the "Current Index."

If the Index is no longer available, the Note Holder will choose a new index which is based upon comparable information. The Note Holder will give me notice of this choice.

(C) Calculation of Changes

Before each Change Date, the Note Holder will calculate my new interest rate by ....

.... percentage points (.................................%) to the Current Index. The result of this calculation:

☐ will not be rounded off.

☐ will be rounded off by the Note Holder to the nearest .... %.

☐ will be rounded off by the Note Holder up to the nearest .... %.

☐ will be rounded off by the Note Holder down to the nearest .... %.

Subject to the limitations stated in Section 4(D) below, this amount will be my new interest rate until the next Change Date.

The Note Holder will then determine the amount of the scheduled payment that would be sufficient to repay the unpaid principal that I am expected to owe at the Change Date in full on the maturity date at my new interest rate in substantially equal payments. The result of this calculation will be the new amount of my scheduled payment.

(D) Limits on Interest Rate Changes

☐ My interest rate will never be increased or decreased on any single change date by more than ....
percentage points from the rate of interest I have been paying for the preceding period.

☐ My interest rate will never be greater than ....% or less than ....%.

(E) Effective Date of Changes

My new interest rate will become effective on each Change Date. I will pay the amount of my new scheduled payment beginning on the first scheduled payment date after the Change Date until the amount of my scheduled payment changes again.

(F) Notice of Changes

At least 25 days, but no more than 120 days, before the effective date of any payment change, the Note Holder will deliver or mail to me a notice of any changes in my interest rate and the amount of my scheduled payment. The notice will include information required by law to be given to me and also the title and telephone number of a person who will answer any question I may have regarding the notice.

5. BORROWER'S RIGHT TO PREPAY

I have the right to make payments of principal at any time before they are due. A payment of principal only is known as a "prepayment." When I make a prepayment, I will tell the Note Holder in writing that I am doing so.

I may make a full prepayment or partial prepayments without paying any prepayment charge. The Note Holder will use all of my prepayments to reduce the amount of principal that I owe under this Note. If I make a partial prepayment, there will be no changes in the due dates of my scheduled payments unless the Note Holder agrees in writing to those changes. My partial prepayment may reduce the amount of my scheduled payments after the first Change Date following my partial prepayment. However, any reduction due to my partial prepayment may be offset by an interest rate increase.

6. LOAN CHARGES

If a law, which applies to this loan and which sets maximum loan charges, is finally interpreted so that the interest or other loan charges collected or to be collected in connection with this loan exceed the permitted limits, then: (i) any such loan charge shall be reduced by the amount necessary to reduce the charge to the permitted limit; and (ii) any sums already collected from me which exceeded permitted limits will be refunded to me. The Note Holder may choose to make this refund by reducing the principal I owe under this Note or by making a direct payment to me. If a refund reduces principal, the reduction will be treated as a partial prepayment.

Form ADJ-NOTE 5/1/91 *(page 2 of 4)*

7. BORROWER'S FAILURE TO PAY AS REQUIRED

(A) Late Charges for Overdue Payments

If the Note Holder has not received the full amount of any scheduled payment by the end of .... calendar days after the date it is due, I will pay a late charge to the Note Holder. The amount of the charge will be ☐ ....% of my overdue payment of principal and interest.   ☐ .... I will pay this late charge promptly but only once on each late payment.

(B) Set-Off

I agree that the Note Holder may set off any amount due and payable under this Note against any right I have to receive money from the Note Holder. An amount due and payable under this Note is any portion of a scheduled payment not paid on or before its due date, even if the due date of the Note has not been accelerated.

My right to receive money from the Note Holder includes any deposit account balance I have with the Note Holder (including savings, checking, and NOW accounts), any time deposit (including certificates of deposit), any money owed to me on an item presented to the Note Holder or in the Note Holder's possession for collection or exchange, and any repurchase agreement or other non-deposit obligation.

If my right to receive money from the Note Holder is also owned by someone who has not agreed to pay this Note, the Note Holder's right of set-off will apply to my interest in the obligation and to any other amounts I could withdraw on my sole request or endorsement. The Note Holder's right of set-off does not apply to an account or other obligation where my rights are only as a fiduciary. It also does not apply to any IRA account or other tax-deferred retirement account.

The Note Holder will not be liable for the dishonor of any check when the dishonor occurs because the Note Holder set off this debt against any of my accounts. I agree to hold the Note Holder harmless from any claims arising as a result of the exercise of the right of set-off.

(C) Default

If I do not pay the full amount of each scheduled payment on the date it is due, I will be in default.

(D) Notice of Default

If I am in default, the Note Holder may send me a written notice telling me that if I do not pay the overdue amount by a certain date, the Note Holder may require me to pay immediately the full amount of principal which has not been paid and all the interest that I owe on that amount. That date must be at least 30 days after the date on which the notice is delivered or mailed to me.

(E) No Waiver By Note Holder

Even if, at a time when I am in default, the Note Holder does not require me to pay immediately in full or does not exercise the right of set-off as described above, the Note Holder will still have the right to do so if I am in default at a later time.

(F) Payment of Note Holder's Costs and Expenses

If the Note Holder has required me to pay immediately in full as described above, the Note Holder will have the right to be paid back by me for all of its costs and expenses in enforcing this Note to the extent not prohibited by applicable law. Those expenses include, for example, reasonable attorneys' fees.

8. GIVING OF NOTICES

Unless applicable law requires a different method, any notice that must be given to me under this Note will be given by delivering it or by mailing it by first class mail to me at the Property Address above or at a different address if I give the Note Holder a notice of my different address.

Any notice that must be given to the Note Holder under this Note will be given by mailing it by first class mail to the Note Holder at the address stated in Section 3(B) above or at a different address if I am given a notice of that different address.

9. OBLIGATIONS OF PERSONS UNDER THIS NOTE

If more than one person signs this Note, each person is fully and personally obligated to keep all of the promises made in this Note, including the promise to pay the full amount owed. Any person who is a guarantor, surety or endorser of this Note is also obligated to do these things. Any person who takes over these obligations, including the obligations of a guarantor, surety or endorser of this Note, is also obligated to keep all of the promises made in this Note. The Note Holder may enforce its rights under this Note against each person individually or against all of us together. This means that any one of us may be required to pay all of the amounts owed under this Note.

10. WAIVERS

I and any other person who has obligations under this Note waive the rights of presentment and notice of dishonor. "Presentment" means the right to require the Note Holder to demand payment of amounts due. "Notice of dishonor" means the right to require the Note Holder to give notice to other persons that amounts due have not been paid.

11. SECURED NOTE

In addition to the protections given to the Note Holder under this Note, a Mortgage, Deed of Trust or Security Deed (the "Security Instrument"), dated the same date as the Note, protects the Note Holder from possible losses which might result if I do not keep the promises which I make in this Note. That Security Instrument describes how and under what conditions I may be required to make immediate payment in full of all amounts I owe under this Note. Some of those conditions are described as follows:

Transfer of the Property or a Beneficial Interest in Borrower. If all or any part of the Property or any interest in it is sold or transferred (or if a beneficial interest in Borrower is sold or transferred and Borrower is not a natural person) without Lender's prior written consent, Lender may, at its option, require immediate payment in full of all sums secured by this Security Instrument. However, this option shall not be exercised by Lender if exercise is prohibited by federal law as of the date of this Security Instrument.

If Lender exercises this option, Lender shall give Borrower notice of acceleration. The notice shall provide a period of not less than 30 days from the date the notice is delivered or mailed within which Borrower must pay all sums secured by this Security Instrument. If Borrower fails to pay these sums prior to the expiration of this period, Lender may invoke any remedies permitted by this Security Instrument without further notice or demand on Borrower.

12. BALLOON PAYMENT DISCLOSURE

[Complete the balloon payment notice below if this Note provides for a balloon payment at Section 3(A) on page 1 of this Note.]

THIS LOAN IS PAYABLE IN FULL ....

.... I MUST REPAY THE ENTIRE PRINCIPAL BALANCE OF THE LOAN AND UNPAID INTEREST THEN DUE, WHICH MAY BE A LARGE PAYMENT. THE LENDER IS UNDER NO OBLIGATION TO REFINANCE THE LOAN AT THAT TIME. I WILL, THEREFORE, BE REQUIRED TO MAKE PAYMENT OUT OF OTHER ASSETS THAT I MAY OWN, OR I WILL HAVE TO FIND A LENDER, WHICH MAY BE THE LENDER I HAVE THIS LOAN WITH, WILLING TO LEND ME THE MONEY. IF I REFINANCE THIS LOAN AT MATURITY, I MAY HAVE TO PAY SOME OR ALL OF THE CLOSING COSTS NORMALLY ASSOCIATED WITH A NEW LOAN EVEN IF I OBTAIN REFINANCING FROM THE SAME LENDER.

WITNESS THE HAND(S) AND SEAL(S) OF THE UNDERSIGNED.

.... (Seal)
-Borrower

.... (Seal)
-Borrower

[Sign Original Only]

Form ADJ-NOTE 5/1/91 *(page 4 of 4)*

NET WORTH STATEMENT

—————— ASSETS ——————

Cash:
    Checking accounts $ _____
    Savings accounts   _____
    Certificates of deposit   _____
    Savings bonds   _____
    Money market accounts   _____
Retirement funds:
    IRA/Keogh accounts   _____
    Pension (vested interest)   _____
Business interests:
    Contracts (money owed you)   _____
Other investments:
    Annuities   _____
    Life insurance (cash value)   _____
    Bonds   _____
    Stocks   _____
    Mutual funds   _____
Personal use assets:
    Home   _____
    Automobiles   _____
    Personal property   _____

TOTAL ASSETS $ _____

—————— LIABILITIES ——————

Credit-card balances:
_____ $ _____
_____   _____

Personal loans:
_____   _____
_____   _____

Business loans:
_____   _____
_____   _____

Mortgages:
_____   _____
_____   _____

Taxes owing:
_____   _____
_____   _____

TOTAL LIABILITIES $ _____

TOTAL ASSETS
LESS TOTAL LIABILITIES   _____

NET WORTH $ _____

CASH FLOW STATEMENT

—————— INCOME ——————

Salary/wages $ _____
Social Security   _____
Pension   _____
Interest/dividends   _____
Reimbursements/refunds   _____
Sale of investments   _____
Alimony/child support   _____
Other:
_____   _____
_____   _____

TOTAL INCOME $ _____

—————— DISTRIBUTIONS ——————

SAVINGS
_____ $ _____
_____   _____

EXPENSES
Income taxes (federal/state)   _____
Property taxes   _____
Insurance (all types)   _____
Medical/dental   _____
Mortgage/rent   _____
Home maintenance/repair   _____
Utilities (including phone)   _____
Debt payments (loans/credit cards):
_____   _____
Food/supermarket items   _____
Restaurants   _____
Recreation   _____
Holiday expenses   _____
Gifts   _____
Education/classes   _____
Clothing/dry cleaning   _____
Expenses for others
   (adult children, etc.)   _____
Newspaper/magazines/books   _____
Subscriptions/dues   _____
Other:
_____   _____
_____   _____

TOTAL DISTRIBUTIONS $ _____

Uniform Residential Loan Application

This application is designed to be completed by the Borrower(s) with the Lender's assistance. The Co-Borrower Section and all other Co-Borrower questions must be completed and the appropriate box(es) checked if ☐ another person will be jointly obligated with the Borrower on the loan, or ☐ the Borrower is relying on income from alimony, child support or separate maintenance or on the income or assets of another person as a basis for repayment of the loan, or ☐ the Borrower is married and resides in, or the property is located in, a community property state.

I. TYPE OF MORTGAGE AND TERMS OF LOAN

Mortgage Applied for:	☐ VA ☐ Conventional ☐ Other:	Agency Case Number	Lender Case No.
	☐ FHA ☐ FmHA		

Amount $	Interest Rate %	No. of Months	Amortization Type:	☐ Fixed Rate ☐ Other (explain):
				☐ GPM ☐ ARM (type):

II. PROPERTY INFORMATION AND PURPOSE OF LOAN

Subject Property Address (street, city, state, & zip code)	No. of Units

Legal Description of Subject Property (attach description if necessary)	Year Built

Purpose of Loan	☐ Purchase ☐ Construction ☐ Other (explain):	Property will be: ☐ Primary Residence ☐ Secondary Residence ☐ Investment
	☐ Refinance ☐ Construction-Permanent	

Complete this line if construction or construction-permanent loan.

Year Lot Acquired	Original Cost $	Amount Existing Liens $	(a) Present Value of Lot $	(b) Cost of Improvements $	Total (a + b) $

Complete this line if this is a refinance loan.

Year Acquired	Original Cost $	Amount Existing Liens $	Purpose of Refinance	Describe Improvements ☐ made ☐ to be made
				Cost: $

Title will be held in what Name(s)	Manner in which Title will be held	Estate will be held in: ☐ Fee Simple ☐ Leasehold (show expiration date)

Source of Down Payment, Settlement Charges and/or Subordinate Financing (explain)

III. BORROWER INFORMATION

Borrower	Co-Borrower

Borrower's Name (include Jr. or Sr. if applicable)	Co-Borrower's Name (include Jr. or Sr. if applicable)

Social Security Number	Home Phone (incl. area code)	Age	Yrs. School	Social Security Number	Home Phone (incl. area code)	Age	Yrs. School

☐ Married ☐ Unmarried (include single, divorced, widowed)	Dependents (not listed by Co-Borrower) no. ages	☐ Married ☐ Unmarried (include single, divorced, widowed)	Dependents (not listed by Borrower) no. ages
☐ Separated		☐ Separated	

Present Address (street, city, state, zip code) ☐ Own ☐ Rent ___ No. Yrs.	Present Address (street, city, state, zip code) ☐ Own ☐ Rent ___ No. Yrs.

If residing at present address for less than seven years, complete the following:

Former Address (street, city, state, zip code)	☐ Own ☐ Rent _____ No. Yrs.	Former Address (street, city, state, zip code)	☐ Own ☐ Rent _____ No. Yrs.
Former Address (street, city, state, zip code)	☐ Own ☐ Rent _____ No. Yrs.	Former Address (street, city, state, zip code)	☐ Own ☐ Rent _____ No. Yrs.

IV. EMPLOYMENT INFORMATION

	Borrower		Co-Borrower	
Name & Address of Employer	☐ Self Employed	Yrs. on this job Yrs. employed in this line of work/profession	Name & Address of Employer	☐ Self Employed	Yrs. on this job Yrs. employed in this line of work/profession
Position/Title/Type of Business	Business Phone (incl. area code)		Position/Title/Type of Business	Business Phone (incl. area code)

If employed in current position for less than two years or if currently employed in more than one position, complete the following:

Name & Address of Employer	☐ Self Employed	Dates (from - to) Monthly Income $	Name & Address of Employer	☐ Self Employed	Dates (from - to) Monthly Income $
Position/Title/Type of Business	Business Phone (incl. area code)		Position/Title/Type of Business	Business Phone (incl. area code)	
Name & Address of Employer	☐ Self Employed	Dates (from - to) Monthly Income $	Name & Address of Employer	☐ Self Employed	Dates (from - to) Monthly Income $
Position/Title/Type of Business	Business Phone (incl. area code)		Position/Title/Type of Business	Business Phone (incl. area code)	

V. MONTHLY INCOME AND COMBINED HOUSING EXPENSE INFORMATION

Gross Monthly Income*	Borrower	Co-Borrower	Total	Combined Monthly Housing Expense	Present	Proposed
Base Empl. Income*	$	$	$	Rent	$	
Overtime				First Mortgage (P&I)		$
Bonuses				Other Financing (P&I)		
Commissions				Hazard Insurance		
Dividends/Interest				Real Estate Taxes		
Net Rental Income				Mortgage Insurance		
Other (before completing, see the notice in "describe other income," below)				Homeowner Assn. Dues		
				Other:		
Total	$	$	$	Total	$	$

* Self Employed Borrower(s) may be required to provide additional documentation such as tax returns and financial statements.

Describe Other Income   *Notice:* Alimony, child support, or separate maintenance income need not be revealed if the Borrower (B) or Co-Borrower (C) does not choose to have it considered for repaying this loan.

B/C		Monthly Amount
		$

VI. ASSETS AND LIABILITIES

This Statement and any applicable supporting schedules may be completed jointly by both married and unmarried Co-Borrowers if their assets and liabilities are sufficiently joined so that the Statement can be meaningfully and fairly presented on a combined basis; otherwise separate Statements and Schedules are required. If the Co-Borrower section was completed about a spouse, this Statement and supporting schedules must be completed about that spouse also.   Completed ☐ Jointly ☐ Not Jointly

ASSETS	Cash or Market Value
Description	$
Cash deposit toward purchase held by:	
List checking and savings accounts below	
Name and address of Bank, S&L, or Credit Union	
Acct. no.	$
Name and address of Bank, S&L, or Credit Union	

Liabilities and Pledged Assets. List the creditor's name, address and account number for all outstanding debts, including automobile loans, revolving charge accounts, real estate loans, alimony, child support, stock pledges, etc. Use continuation sheet, if necessary. Indicate by (*) those liabilities which will be satisfied upon sale of real estate owned or upon refinancing of the subject property.

LIABILITIES	Monthly Payt. & Mos. Left to Pay	Unpaid Balance
Name and address of Company	$ Payt./Mos.	$
Acct. no.		
Name and address of Company	$ Payt./Mos.	$
Acct. no.		
Name and address of Company	$ Payt./Mos.	$

Assets (Total Assets a.)

Acct. no.
Name and address of Bank, S&L, or Credit Union
$

Acct. no.
Name and address of Bank, S&L, or Credit Union
$

Acct. no.
Stocks & Bonds (Company name/number & description)
$

Life insurance net cash value
$
Face amount: $

Subtotal Liquid Assets
$

Real estate owned (enter market value from schedule of real estate owned)
$

Vested interest in retirement fund
$

Net worth of business(es) owned (attach financial statement)
$

Automobiles owned (make and year)
$

Other Assets (itemize)
$

Total Assets a. $

Liabilities (Total Liabilities b.)

Acct. no.
Name and address of Company
$ Payt./Mos.
$

Acct. no.
Name and address of Company
$ Payt./Mos.
$

Acct. no.
Name and address of Company
$ Payt./Mos.
$

Acct. no.
Name and address of Company
$ Payt./Mos.
$

Acct. no.
Alimony/Child Support/Separate Maintenance Payments Owed to:
$

Job Related Expense (child care, union dues, etc.)
$

Total Monthly Payments
$

Net Worth (a minus b)
$

Total Liabilities b.
$

VI. ASSETS AND LIABILITIES (cont.)

Schedule of Real Estate Owned (If additional properties are owned, use continuation sheet.)

Property Address (enter S if sold, PS if pending sale or R if rental being held for income)	Type of Property	Present Market Value	Amount of Mortgages & Liens	Gross Rental Income	Mortgage Payments	Insurance, Maintenance, Taxes & Misc.	Net Rental Income
		$	$	$	$	$	$
Totals		$	$			$	$

List any additional names under which credit has previously been received and indicate appropriate creditor name(s) and account number(s):

Alternate Name	Creditor Name	Account Number

VII. DETAILS OF TRANSACTION

a. Purchase price $

b. Alterations, improvements, repairs

c. Land (if acquired separately)

d. Refinance (incl. debts to be paid off)

e. Estimated prepaid items

f. Estimated closing costs

g. PMI, MIP, Funding Fee paid in cash

h. Discount (if Borrower will pay)

i. **Total costs (add items a through h)**

j. Subordinate financing

k. Borrower's closing costs paid by Seller

l. Other Credits (explain)

m. Loan amount (exclude PMI, MIP, Funding Fee financed)

n. PMI, MIP, Funding Fee financed

o. Loan amount (add m & n)

p. Cash from/to Borrower (subtract j, k, l & o from i)

VIII. DECLARATIONS

If you answer "yes" to any questions a through i, please use continuation sheet for explanation.

	Borrower Yes	Borrower No	Co-Borrower Yes	Co-Borrower No
a. Are there any outstanding judgments against you?	☐	☐	☐	☐
b. Have you been declared bankrupt within the past 7 years?	☐	☐	☐	☐
c. Have you had property foreclosed upon or given title or deed in lieu thereof in the last 7 years?	☐	☐	☐	☐
d. Are you a party to a law suit?	☐	☐	☐	☐
e. Have you directly or indirectly been obligated on any loan which resulted in foreclosure, transfer of title in lieu of foreclosure, or judgment? (This would include such loans as home mortgage loans, SBA loans, home improvement loans, educational loans, manufactured (mobile) home loans, any mortgage, financial obligation, bond, or loan guarantee. If "Yes," provide details, including date, name and address of Lender, FHA or VA case number, if any, and reasons for the action.)	☐	☐	☐	☐
f. Are you presently delinquent or in default on any Federal debt or any other loan, mortgage, financial obligation, bond, or loan guarantee? If "Yes," give details as described in the preceding question.	☐	☐	☐	☐
g. Are you obligated to pay alimony, child support, or separate maintenance?	☐	☐	☐	☐
h. Is any part of the down payment borrowed?	☐	☐	☐	☐
i. Are you a co-maker or endorser on a note?	☐	☐	☐	☐
j. Are you a U.S. citizen?	☐	☐	☐	☐
k. Are you a permanent resident alien?	☐	☐	☐	☐
l. Do you intend to occupy the property as your primary residence?	☐	☐	☐	☐

IX. ACKNOWLEDGMENT AND AGREEMENT

The undersigned specifically acknowledge(s) and agree(s) that: (1) the loan requested by this application will be secured by a first mortgage or deed of trust on the property described herein; (2) the property will not be used for any illegal or prohibited purpose or use; (3) all statements made in this application are made for the purpose of obtaining the loan indicated herein; (4) occupation of the property will be as indicated above; (5) verification or reverification of any information contained in the application may be made at any time by the Lender, its agents, successors and assigns, either directly or through a credit reporting agency, from any source named in this application, and the original copy of this application will be retained by the Lender, even if the loan is not approved; (6) the Lender, its agents, successors and assigns will rely on the information contained in the application and I/we have a continuing obligation to amend and/or supplement the information provided in this application if any of the material facts which I/we have represented herein should change prior to closing; (7) in the event my/our payments on the loan indicated in this application become delinquent, the Lender, its agents, successors and assigns, may, in addition to all their other rights and remedies, report my/our name(s) and account information to a credit reporting agency; (8) ownership of the loan may be transferred to successor or assign of the Lender without notice to me and/or the administration of the loan account may be transferred to an agent, successor or assign of the Lender with prior notice to me; (9) the Lender, its agents, successors and assigns make no representations or warranties, express or implied, to the Borrower(s) regarding the property, the condition of the property, or the value of the property.

Certification: I/We certify that the information provided in this application is true and correct as of the date set forth opposite my/our signature(s) on this application and acknowledge my/our understanding that any intentional or negligent misrepresentation(s) of the information contained in this application may result in civil liability and/or criminal penalties including, but not limited to, fine or imprisonment or both under the provisions of Title 18, United States Code, Section 1001, et seq. and liability for monetary damages to the Lender, its agents, successors and assigns, insurers and any other person who may suffer any loss due to reliance upon any misrepresentation which I/we have made on this application.

Borrower's Signature	Date
X	

Co-Borrower's Signature	Date
X	

X. INFORMATION FOR GOVERNMENT MONITORING PURPOSES

The following information is requested by the Federal Government for certain types of loans related to a dwelling, in order to monitor the Lender's compliance with equal credit opportunity, fair housing and home mortgage disclosure laws. You are not required to furnish this information, but are encouraged to do so. The law provides that a Lender may neither discriminate on the basis of this information, nor on whether you choose to furnish it. However, if you choose not to furnish it, under Federal regulations this Lender is required to note race and sex on the basis of visual observation or surname. If you do not wish to furnish the above information, please check the box below. (Lender must review the above material to assure that the disclosures satisfy all requirements to which the Lender is subject under applicable state law for the particular type of loan applied for.)

BORROWER

☐ I do not wish to furnish this information

Race/National Origin:
☐ American Indian or Alaskan Native
☐ Asian or Pacific Islander
☐ Black, not of Hispanic origin
☐ White, not of Hispanic origin
☐ Hispanic

Sex:
☐ Female
☐ Male

CO-BORROWER

☐ I do not wish to furnish this information

Race/National Origin:
☐ American Indian or Alaskan Native
☐ Asian or Pacific Islander
☐ Black, not of Hispanic origin
☐ White, not of Hispanic origin
☐ Hispanic

Sex:
☐ Female
☐ Male

To be Completed by Interviewer

This application was taken by:
☐ face-to-face interview
☐ by mail
☐ by telephone

Interviewer's Name (print or type)	Name and Address of Interviewer's Employer
Interviewer's Signature	Date
Interviewer's Phone Number (incl. area code)	

I/We fully understand that it is a Federal crime punishable by fine or imprisonment, or both, to knowingly make any false statements concerning any of the above facts as applicable under the provisions of Title 18, United States Code, Section 1001, et seq.

Borrower's Signature	Date
X	

Co-Borrower's Signature	Date
X	

BORROWER'S NAME AND ADDRESS

LENDER'S NAME AND ADDRESS

Loan Number _____
Date _____
Mat. Date _____
Loan Amount $ _____

TRUTH-IN-LENDING DISCLOSURES
"I" MEANS THE BORROWER AND "YOU" MEANS THE LENDER

ANNUAL PERCENTAGE RATE The cost of my credit as a yearly rate.	FINANCE CHARGE The dollar amount the credit will cost me.	AMOUNT FINANCED The amount of credit provided to me or on my behalf.	TOTAL OF PAYMENTS The amount I will have paid when I have made all scheduled payments.
____ %	$ ____	$ ____	$ ____

I have the right to receive at this time an itemization of the Amount Financed
I ____ do ____ do not want an itemization.

My Payment Schedule will be:

Number of Payments	Amount of Payments	When Payments Are Due
	$	
	$	
	$	
	$	
	$	
	$	

Demand: ☐ This loan has a demand feature. ☐ This loan is payable on demand and all disclosures are based on an assumed maturity of one year.

Variable Rate: (check one below)
☐ My loan contains a variable rate feature. Disclosures about the variable rate feature have been provided to me earlier.
☐ The annual percentage rate may increase during the term of this transaction if _____.

Any increase will take the form of _____.
If the rate increases by ____ % in _____, the _____.
will increase to _____. The rate may not increase more often than once
and may not increase more than ____ % each _____. The rate will not go above ____ %.

Security: I am giving a security interest in:
☐ the goods or property being purchased.
☐ _____ (brief description of other property)
☐ collateral securing other loans with you may also secure this loan.
☐ my deposit accounts and other rights I may have to the payment of money from you.

Late Charge: If a payment is late I will be charged _____.

Prepayment: If I pay off this loan early, I
☐ may ☐ will not have to pay a penalty.
☐ may ☐ will not be entitled to a refund of part of the finance charge.

Filing/Recording Fees: $ _____

Assumption: Someone buying my house ☐ may, subject to conditions, be allowed to ☐ cannot assume the remainder of the mortgage on the original terms.

I can see my contract documents for any additional information about nonpayment, default, any required repayment in full before the scheduled date, and prepayment refunds and penalties.   "e" means an estimate.

CREDIT INSURANCE - Credit life insurance and credit disability insurance are not required to obtain credit, and will not be provided unless I sign and agree to pay the additional costs.

Type	Premium	Term
Credit Life		
Credit Disability		
Joint Credit Life		

I ☐ do ☐ do not want credit life insurance.

X _____ DOB _____

I ☐ do ☐ do not want credit disability insurance.

X _____ DOB _____

I ☐ do ☐ do not want joint credit life insurance.

X _____ DOB _____

I ☐ do ☐ do not want _____ insurance.

X _____ DOB _____

PROPERTY INSURANCE - I may obtain property insurance from anyone I want that is acceptable to you. If I get the insurance from or through you I will pay

$ _____ for _____ of coverage.

FLOOD INSURANCE - Flood insurance ☐ is ☐ is not required. I may obtain flood insurance from anyone I want that is acceptable to you. If I get the insurance from or through you I will pay

$ _____ for _____ of coverage.

ITEMIZATION OF AMOUNT FINANCED

Amount given to me directly	$ _____
Amount paid on my (loan) account	$ _____

AMOUNTS PAID TO OTHERS ON MY BEHALF:

Insurance Companies	$ _____
Public Officials	$ _____
	$ _____
	$ _____
	$ _____
	$ _____
	$ _____
	$ _____
	$ _____
	$ _____
	$ _____
	$ _____
	$ _____
	$ _____
(less) PREPAID FINANCE CHARGE(S)	$ _____
Amount Financed	$ _____

(Add all items financed and subtract prepaid finance charges.)

BY SIGNING BELOW - I ACKNOWLEDGE RECEIPT OF A COPY OF THIS DISCLOSURE ON THE DATE INDICATED ABOVE.

X _____   X _____

Truth-in-Lending Statement
Copyright © 1991, Bankers Systems, Inc., St. Cloud, MN.

LOAN COMMITMENT

APPLICANT'S NAME AND CURRENT ADDRESS	LENDER'S NAME AND ADDRESS	Loan Number _____ Date of Application _____ Date of Commitment _____ Commitment Expires _____

We have received your application and are issuing this Loan Commitment based on the terms and conditions listed below and on page 2 for the property located at _____.

Loan Purpose: ☐ Purchase   ☐ Refinance   Loan Plan _____   Date of Loan Approval _____

Lien Priority: ☐ First   ☐ Second   ☐ Other

Occupancy: ☐ Owner-Occupied   ☐ Second Home   ☐ Investor

Loan Terms:
Purchase Price $ _____ (if applicable)   Minimum Appraised Value $ _____
Loan Amount $ _____   Loan Term _____ (months) Loan to Value (LTV) _____ %
Interest Rate _____ % (Initial Rate if Adjustable)   Principal & Interest (P&I) $ _____

Loan Type: ☐ Fixed Rate   ☐ Adjustable Rate (_____ Index Value _____ Margin)
☐ Balloon   ☐ Temporary Buydown   ☐ Other
Please refer to the Truth in Lending disclosure for the repayment schedule.

Property Type: ☐ Single Family   ☐ 2-4 Units   ☐ Townhouse   ☐ Condominium   ☐ Other

Loan Fees:
Origination Fee _____ % of Loan Amount or $ _____   Application Fee $ _____
Discount Points _____ % of Loan Amount or $ _____   Credit Report $ _____
Appraisal $ _____ Other _____ $ _____

This does not constitute all the fees that will be paid at closing. Please consult your Good Faith Estimate or request a schedule of fees from the Lender for your loan transaction. Some or all of these fees may not be refundable if your loan does not close.

☐ **Commitment Fee:** _____ % of the loan amount or $ _____ .
   ☐ The commitment fee will be applied to closing costs at time of closing.
   ☐ The commitment fee is refundable.
   ☐ The commitment fee is non-refundable and will not be applied to closing costs at time of closing.

☐ **Private Mortgage Insurance**
   Depending upon your loan to value ratio, the Lender may require private mortgage insurance. The insurance coverage and private mortgage insurance company must be acceptable to the Lender.

☐ **Additional Provisions**

_____
_____
_____
_____

Additional Requirements - please provide to Lender.

☐ Signed purchase contract
☐ Construction loan agreement
☐ Survey or improvement location certificate acceptable to Lender
☐ Final inspection for repairs or completion of construction acceptable to Lender
☐ Well and/or septic certifications acceptable to Lender
☐ Real estate appraisal acceptable to Lender
☐ Other: _____
☐ Other: _____
☐ Other: _____
☐ Other: _____
☐ Other: _____

See page 2   Page 2 contains additional information and is made a part of this Loan Commitment.

Instructions: Please sign and return the Lender's copy of this Loan Commitment to the above address of the Lender. If this Loan Commitment is not accepted and returned to the Lender by _____, the Loan Commitment will become void and invalid.

Dated: _____   By _____   _____ Lender's authorized signature

We, the Applicant(s) and Seller(s), if applicable, understand and accept the conditions and the terms stated above and on page 2.

_____ _____   _____ _____
Applicant   Date   Seller   Date

_____ _____   _____ _____
Applicant   Date   Seller   Date

ADDITIONAL TERMS OF THE LOAN COMMITMENT

VA, FHA or FmHA INSURED LOANS

The Applicant(s) and the Lender must comply with all the agency rules and regulations of the Department of Veterans Affairs, the Federal Housing Administration, or the Farmers Home Administration, if applicable.

TITLE INSURANCE

Title to the property listed on page 1 must be acceptable to Lender. Lender must be furnished with a title insurance policy issued by a company satisfactory to Lender, with such policy naming the Lender as the insured party for the amount of the loan (or other amount to which the Lender may agree in writing). The policy must insure the security instrument to have the lien priority indicated on page 1, free from all exceptions except those approved by Lender. The Lender, at its option, may accept an attorney's opinion instead of a title insurance policy.

HAZARD AND FLOOD INSURANCE

At loan closing the Lender must be furnished with a hazard insurance policy covering the property listed on page 1 against loss by fire and other hazards as are customary in the area in which the property is located. If the property is located in a flood hazard area then flood insurance is required under the National Flood Insurance Act of 1968, as amended. The hazard insurance policy and flood insurance policy (if required) must be in an amount not less than the amount of the loan (or other amount to which the Lender may agree in writing). The insurance policies shall be in a form acceptable to the Lender and shall have a loss payee provision acceptable to the Lender, its successors and/or assigns.

LOAN DOCUMENTATION

The security instrument and other loan documents will be provided by the Lender and must be signed by all Applicant(s). A non-applicant spouse may be required to sign the security instrument if the signature is necessary to relinquish his or her rights in the property.

ESCROW OR IMPOUND ACCOUNTS

The Lender may require additional deposits to establish and maintain escrow or impound accounts. These accounts will be used to pay such items (if applicable) as real estate taxes, hazard insurance, private mortgage insurance, FHA mortgage insurance premiums, and other items that the Lender may require.

CANCELLATION

The Lender has the right to cancel this Loan Commitment if the financial status of the Applicant(s) is adversely affected or the property listed on page 1 is damaged by fire, flood or other casualty. If the loan is not made through no fault of the Lender, the Applicant(s) shall reimburse the Lender for any expenses incurred by the Lender on behalf of the Applicant(s) in the preparation of the funding of the loan, including but not limited to an attorney's opinion or title commitment, tax statements, survey, inspections, credit reports, appraisal or other charges that are actually incurred. These charges shall be in addition to any non-refundable commitment fee paid by the Applicant(s).

NEW CONSTRUCTION

The Applicant(s) must provide the Lender with the appropriate plans and specifications for the property. Any changes to the plans and specifications must be approved by the Lender in writing. All work performed must comply with the plans and specifications, conform to applicable building codes, and be done in a good and workman-like manner. The completed work must be approved by the Lender. The Applicant(s) will provide the Lender with paid receipts and lien waivers for all work done and all materials provided.

— 12 —
Settlement

Terri and her friend, Sarah, decided to buy a house together. They believed that it would be better financially for both of them. Instead of renting, they would build equity in a house of their own. They were pleased that everything was going well and on schedule. On settlement day, one hour before their meeting, they walked through the property. To their surprise, the house was still full of furniture belonging to the owner. They were advised not to settle until the owner had moved out. They refused to settle and asked to reschedule the meeting for settlement for the following week to allow the owner additional time to move out. Did Terri and Sarah make the right decision?

Terri and Sarah were well advised to postpone settlement. They can call the shots here. They are in compliance with the Agreement of Sale and are ready to perform, while the seller is not. Remember: If they settle now, they will inherit a tenant they do not want in their house!

It may seem like a very long time since you began your journey toward home ownership. After all, you had a lot to learn and a lot to do before you could feel confident with this decision. Now you are ready to prepare yourself for settlement, the day that you take title to your new home!

IMPORTANT POINTS TO ESTABLISH BEFORE SETTLEMENT

Just before settlement, you should make sure that the following items have been taken care of or established. Double check that the legal description of the property is what it is supposed to be. By this time, your Realtor should know that there are no title defects and that all liens (mechanic's, materialman's, and/or child support in some states) have been satisfied. Your lender should have received the credit report and contacted you if there were any questions about it. Either the lender or your Realtor should have the results of the appraisal (which the lender ordered) by now.

Homeowner's Insurance

Before the day of settlement, if you are getting a conventional mortgage loan, you should contact an insurance agent to arrange for homeowner's insurance to be issued as of the date of settlement with the lender named Beneficiary. This is required of all buyers who have a conventional mortgage. The amount of insurance need only be enough to cover the mortgage. For example, if you agree to buy the house for $85,000 and put 10% down, your mortgage will be $76,500. However, consider the replacement value of the home in the event of a fire or other major damage, then decide on the amount of insurance you wish to carry on the house. Also be sure to check on the necessity for flood, earthquake, or other natural disaster insurance. Discuss the best package of coverage with your insurance agent.

Utilities

Be sure to notify the utility companies that you will want the service put into your name as of the date of settlement. For example, you will need electric, water, gas or oil, and telephone service. Although some services, such as water, will be notified through the settlement process, take the responsibility and do it yourself. If this is your first home and you are a new account with the utility company, you may have to put a deposit down on the service requested. You may also have to fill out a credit application. Do not leave these important tasks go until the last minute. Many times these deposits are refunded after a year or so of good payment history with the utility company.

THE WALK-THROUGH

You should definitely make a pre-settlement walk-through in your home-to-be. You should be sure that all is in order in the house as agreed to in the sales contract. Check that all contingencies have been fulfilled, especially any conditions you required changed as a result of the inspection. If you have any questions, raise them before any papers are signed at the settlement table.

For example, the seller may have agreed to leave two window air conditioners in the house. When you walk through, you do not see either air conditioner. What can you do? You can negotiate for the amount of money needed to buy two window air conditioners; you can insist on the two window air conditioners before you sign anything at the closing; or you can consider the seller to be in breach of contract and refuse to settle. The lawyers will do everything possible to negotiate the contract between the parties so that a settlement can take place on schedule. Buyer beware! Take the time to do a walk-through before you settle on the property. What if the owner has not yet moved the furniture out of the house before settlement? You have a choice. You can settle and inherit a tenant that may or may not leave the premises easily. You can postpone settlement for a short time to allow the owner to move out. Consult your lawyer if you meet up with this situation.

SETTLEMENT DAY

In addition, you should sit down the day before settlement with your lawyer or Realtor. Go over the settlement sheet so that you are prepared to pay the required charges and fees. (Your lawyer may have to call you at the last minute before settlement to give you the exact amount for which the check should be made out. This is because of the prorated fees, which may change daily.) You will need to pay the settlement amount with a certified check or cashier's check. (A credit union check is also usually acceptable. Ask your lawyer.) Certified checks are available at any bank.

The Buyer's Settlement Cost Sheet example given below details the items for which you will be charged at settlement.

The Deed

Your lender (bank, savings and loan, or mortgage company) or full service Realtor will have prepared the deed, mortgage, note, and in some cases, the title insurance for signatures at settlement.

Be sure the deed is written the way you specified. Look over it carefully. If you want to take title as a sole owner, then look at the top of the deed where it describes the transfer from the seller to you, the buyer. Does it state your name correctly? Your name should be followed by one of the following terms: (1) tenant in common; (2) tenant in common or joint tenant with right of survivorship; (3) tenancy by the entirety; (4) grantee and his/her heirs, (often used for a single woman or single man, and serves the same purpose as tenants in common).

Each of these statements above (1-4) will be legally interpreted in case of your death to determine what you intended would happen to your property in your estate. Be sure you have thought about this. If all is as you requested, you will sign the deed.

Mortgage Note

The mortgage note specifies the conditions of your mortgage loan and secures it against the property you are buying. The lender sets out the conditions of the repayment terms here. Read this carefully and ask questions if you are unclear about these conditions. The lender should have gone over these terms when you agreed to the loan. Once you sign the note, it is legally binding until it is paid in full. In it, you promise to pay the agreed amount over a set number of months at a stated interest rate. If you break your promise, the lender has the legal right to call in your loan. If that happens, it is likely that your lender will begin foreclosure proceedings. No one wants this to happen. It is for this reason that lenders are so tough in the beginning of the loan qualifying process. They want your business but only if they are sure you will follow-through and keep up your payments.

Title Insurance

Although title insurance is optional in some states, it is good protection against a "cloud on the title" of your home. It insures you that the title is clear and free of all known defects and liens. Common title defects include tax liens, and mechanic's and materialman's liens. A tax lien may be placed on a property when property taxes have not been paid. A mechanic's lien takes effect when a contractor who has done work on the property has not been paid. A materialman's lien is similar but involves unpaid suppliers or vendors of materials.

The purpose of title insurance is to determine that all mortgages and other forms of liens have been paid in full and are no longer secured by the property you are buying. You will pay approximately $50 per thousand dollars of mortgage. For example, if you get an $85,000 mortgage, you will probably pay $425 for title insurance.

Recording the Deed

The lawyer, whether it is your lawyer or the lender's lawyer, will file all the necessary forms needed to record the deed at the courthouse following the settlement. The transaction will now be of public record. Across the United States, there are some variations on the types of real property ownership. The following chart indicates the types applicable in each state.

If all the paperwork is in order, everyone arrives on time for the appointment, and no further hitches ensue, a settlement will take approximately thirty to sixty minutes. You will leave as the new homeowner.

Make sure you don't leave the closing appointment without the keys to your new home. You may have to have your lawyer hold up the closing process to get them. The last thing you want is to have signed all the papers, handed over a large amount of money, and heaved a sigh of relief, only to find you cannot get into the property!

Congratulations! Enjoy your new home.

QUICK CHECKLIST SETTLEMENT DAY

1. Have you seen the completed Buyer's Settlement Cost sheet and are you aware of the items to be paid at settlement?

2. Have you planned to walk through the property before settlement?

3. Have you planned to confirm the final amount with your attorney a day or so before closing so you can get the cashier's check for the appropriate amount?

4. Have you arranged for homeowner's insurance, naming your lender as beneficiary?

5. Did you notify the utility companies to transfer accounts into your name as of the date of settlement?

6. Did you check the deed to be sure it is written the way you specified?

7. Is the mortgage note as you expected?

8. Is the title insurance complete?

9. Is your lawyer satisfied that all the details are in order?

10. Are all conditions of the Agreement of Sale in order?

Statement of Estimated Buyers' Costs

This form recommended and approved for, but not restricted to, use by members of the Greater Harrisburg Association of REALTORS®

DATE PREPARED _____

PREPARED BY _____
            Salesperson

BUYER _____

PROPERTY _____

The following is provided so that the Buyers will understand approximately what costs will be required of them on or before the date of settlement.

Sale Price .... $ _____

Down Payment (incl. deposit) $ _____

Mortgage Amount .... $ _____

Type of Financing _____

Estimate of Monthly Payment:

At _____ % interest if year loan is granted.

Principal and Interest .... $ _____

PMI Premium .... $ _____

Tax Escrow .... $ _____

Homeowners Insurance Escrow .... $ _____

TOTAL PAYMENT .... $ _____

Estimate of Monthly Payment:

At _____ % interest if year loan is granted.

Principal and Interest .... $ _____

PMI Premium .... $ _____

Tax Escrow .... $ _____

Homeowners Insurance Escrow .... $ _____

TOTAL PAYMENT .... $ _____

1. Mortgage Application/Appraisal Fee/Credit Report $ _____
2. Lender's Service/Mortgage Placement Fee ...... $ _____
3. Interest on Mortgage ...... $ _____
4. Mortgage Insurance Premium .... $ _____
5. VA Funding Fee .... $ _____
6. Tax Escrow/Proration (14 months' taxes) ...... $ _____
7. Tax Service Fee .... $ _____
8. Document Preparation .... $ _____
9. Mortgage Assumption Fee .... $ _____
10. Homeowner's Insurance Policy (First Year Premium) .... $ _____
    Two (2) month's escrow to lender ...... $ _____
11. Title Search/Insurance and Endorsements ...... $ _____
12. Recording of Deed .... $ _____
13. Recording of Mortgage .... $ _____
14. Transfer Tax _____ % of $ _____ ...... $ _____
15. Notary Fees .... $ _____
16. Home Warranty Plan .... $ _____
17. Lot Survey .... $ _____
18. Radon Test .... $ _____
19. Well Water Analysis Report .... $ _____
20. Wood Infestation Report .... $ _____
21. Private On-Lot Sewage System Inspection ...... $ _____

22. Real Estate Commission/Compensation .... $ _____   SETTLEMENT COSTS ... $ _____
23. _____ $ _____   Down Payment (incl. deposit) $ _____
24. _____ $ _____   TOTAL AMOUNT NEEDED .... $ _____

SETTLEMENT COSTS ....

Except as may be provided by an addendum to the Agreement of Sale, THE AGENT REPRESENTS THE SELLER; however, the agent may perform services for the Buyer in connection with financing, insurance, and document preparation.

These are approximate figures. Exact figures will be provided at the time of settlement.

A Certified Check or Cashier's Check is required at settlement.

I/We hereby acknowledge receipt of a copy of this Statement of Estimated Buyers' Settlement Costs and Estimate of Monthly Payments, and approve the above Estimated Charges.

I/We further understand that the above costs are estimated and based on the best information available at this date and that they are subject to changes, particularly in the case of the escrow charges such as taxes, water and sewage, rent and insurance.

I/We hereby acknowledge receipt of a copy of the Disclosure Regarding Real Estate Agency Relationship,

DEPOSIT MONEY: NOTICE TO THE BUYER(S):

1. The Selling Broker is _____, who is the Subagent for the Seller (except as may be provided by an addendum to the Agreement of Sale) and will accept your sales deposit for transfer to the Listing Broker, _____, who is Agent for the Seller.

2. The Agent for the Seller is a Pennsylvania licensed real estate broker who is required to hold your sales deposit in escrow.

3. If your deposit is in the form of a check or a note, it is to be made payable to the Agent for the Seller.

4. The undersigned acknowledge receipt of this notice prior to signing the Agreement of Sale.

Fax Statement: This Document and any amendments thereto, may be executed in multiple counterparts by the parties and delivered by way of transmission through a facsimile (FAX) machine and such counterparts shall have the same legal enforceability and binding effect as though it were signed by all parties in original form.

WITNESS _____   BUYER(S): _____   DATE: _____

WITNESS _____   BUYER(S): _____   DATE: _____

By permission of Greater Harrisburg Association of Realtors, 1992.

NOTE

.............., 19.........

...................................., ...
[City]   [State]

....
[Property Address]

1. BORROWER'S PROMISE TO PAY

In return for a loan that I have received, I promise to pay U.S. $................ (this amount is called "principal"), plus interest, to the order of the Lender. The Lender is .... I understand that the Lender may transfer this Note. The Lender or anyone who takes this Note by transfer and who is entitled to receive payments under this Note is called the "Note Holder."

2. INTEREST

Interest will be charged on unpaid principal until the full amount of principal has been paid. I will pay interest at a yearly rate of ....%.

The interest rate required by this Section 2 is the rate I will pay both before and after any default described in Section 6(B) of this Note.

3. PAYMENTS

(A) Time and Place of Payments

I will pay principal and interest by making payments every month.

I will make my monthly payments on the .... day of each month beginning on ...., 19........ I will make these payments every month until I have paid all of the principal and interest and any other charges described below that I may owe under this Note. My monthly payments will be applied to interest before principal. If, on ...., I still owe amounts under this Note, I will pay those amounts in full on that date, which is called the "maturity date."

I will make my monthly payments at .... or at a different place if required by the Note Holder.

(B) Amount of Monthly Payments

My monthly payment will be in the amount of U.S. $..

4. BORROWER'S RIGHT TO PREPAY

I have the right to make payments of principal at any time before they are due. A payment of principal only is known as a "prepayment." When I make a prepayment, I will tell the Note Holder in writing that I am doing so.

I may make a full prepayment or partial prepayments without paying any prepayment charge. The Note Holder will use all of my prepayments to reduce the amount of principal that I owe under this Note. If I make a partial prepayment, there will be no changes in the due date or in the amount of my monthly payment unless the Note Holder agrees in writing to those changes.

5. LOAN CHARGES

If a law, which applies to this loan and which sets maximum loan charges, is finally interpreted so that the interest or other loan charges collected or to be collected in connection with this loan exceed the permitted limits, then: (i) any such loan charge shall be reduced by the amount necessary to reduce the charge to the permitted limit; and (ii) any sums already collected from me which exceeded permitted limits will be refunded to me. The Note Holder may choose to make this refund by reducing the principal I owe under this Note or by making a direct payment to me. If a refund reduces principal, the reduction will be treated as a partial prepayment.

6. BORROWER'S FAILURE TO PAY AS REQUIRED

(A) Late Charge for Overdue Payments

If the Note Holder has not received the full amount of any monthly payment by the end of .... calendar days after the date it is due, I will pay a late charge to the Note Holder. The amount of the charge will be ....% of my overdue payment of principal and interest. I will pay this late charge promptly but only once on each late payment.

(B) Default

If I do not pay the full amount of each monthly payment on the date it is due, I will be in default.

(C) Notice of Default

If I am in default, the Note Holder may send me a written notice telling me that if I do not pay the overdue amount by a certain date, the Note Holder may require me to pay immediately the full amount of principal which has not been paid and all the interest that I owe on that amount. That date must be at least 30 days after the date on which the notice is delivered or mailed to me.

(D) No Waiver By Note Holder

Even if, at a time when I am in default, the Note Holder does not require me to pay immediately in full as described above, the Note Holder will still have the right to do so if I am in default at a later time.

(E) Payment of Note Holder's Costs and Expenses

If the Note Holder has required me to pay immediately in full as described above, the Note Holder will have the right to be paid back by me for all of its costs and expenses in enforcing this Note to the extent not prohibited by applicable law. Those expenses include, for example, reasonable attorneys' fees.

7. GIVING OF NOTICES

Unless applicable law requires a different method, any notice that must be given to me under this Note will be given by delivering it or by mailing it by first class mail to me at the Property Address above or at a different address if I give the Note Holder a notice of my different address.

Any notice that must be given to the Note Holder under this Note will be given by mailing it by first class mail to the Note Holder at the address stated in Section 3(A) above or at a different address if I am given a notice of that different address.

8. OBLIGATIONS OF PERSONS UNDER THIS NOTE

If more than one person signs this Note, each person is fully and personally obligated to keep all of the promises made in this Note, including the promise to pay the full amount owed. Any person who is a guarantor, surety or endorser of this Note is also obligated to do these things. Any person who takes over these obligations, including the obligations of a guarantor, surety or endorser of this Note, is also obligated to keep all of the promises made in this Note. The Note Holder may enforce its rights under this Note against each person individually or against all of us together. This means that any one of us may be required to pay all of the amounts owed under this Note.

9. WAIVERS

I and any other person who has obligations under this Note waive the rights of presentment and notice of dishonor. "Presentment" means the right to require the Note Holder to demand payment of amounts due. "Notice of dishonor" means the right to require the Note Holder to give notice to other persons that amounts due have not been paid.

10. UNIFORM SECURED NOTE

This Note is a uniform instrument with limited variations in some jurisdictions. In addition to the protections given to the Note Holder under this Note, a Mortgage, Deed of Trust or Security Deed (the "Security Instrument"), dated the same date as this Note, protects the Note Holder from possible losses which might result if I do not keep the promises which I make in this Note. That Security Instrument describes how and under what conditions I may be required to make immediate payment in full of all amounts I owe under this Note. Some of those conditions are described as follows:

Transfer of the Property or a Beneficial Interest in Borrower. If all or any part of the Property or any interest in it is sold or transferred (or if a beneficial interest in Borrower is sold or transferred and Borrower is not a natural person) without Lender's prior written consent, Lender may, at its option, require immediate payment in full of all sums secured by this Security Instrument. However, this option shall not be exercised by Lender if exercise is prohibited by federal law as of the date of this Security Instrument.

If Lender exercises this option, Lender shall give Borrower notice of acceleration. The notice shall provide a period of not less than 30 days from the date the notice is delivered or mailed within which Borrower must pay all sums secured by this Security Instrument. If Borrower fails to pay these sums prior to the expiration of this period, Lender may invoke any remedies permitted by this Security Instrument without further notice or demand on Borrower.

WITNESS THE HAND(S) AND SEAL(S) OF THE UNDERSIGNED.

....(Seal)
-Borrower

....(Seal)
-Borrower

....(Seal)
-Borrower

[Sign Original Only]

Commonwealth.
Land Title Insurance Company

POLICY NUMBER

OWNER'S POLICY OF TITLE INSURANCE

SUBJECT TO THE EXCLUSIONS FROM COVERAGE, THE EXCEPTIONS CONTAINED IN SCHEDULE B AND THE PROVISIONS OF THE CONDITIONS AND STIPULATIONS HEREOF, COMMONWEALTH LAND TITLE INSURANCE COMPANY, a Pennsylvania corporation, herein called the Company, insures, as of Date of Policy shown in Schedule A, against loss or damage, not exceeding the amount of insurance stated in Schedule A, and cost, attorneys' fees and expenses which the Company may become obligated to pay hereunder, sustained or incurred by the insured by reason of:

1. Title to the estate or interest described in Schedule A being vested otherwise than as stated therein;
2. Any defect in or lien or encumbrance on such title;
3. Lack of a right of access to and from the land; or
4. Unmarketability of such title.

IN WITNESS WHEREOF, the Commonwealth Land Title Insurance Company has caused its corporate name and seal to be hereunto affixed by its duly authorized officers, the policy to become valid when countersigned by an authorized officer or agent of the Company.

COMMONWEALTH LAND TITLE INSURANCE COMPANY

Attest: *James J.D. Lynch Jr*   Secretary

By *Frederick Saville*   President

EXCLUSIONS FROM COVERAGE

The following matters are expressly excluded from the coverage of this policy:

1. (a) Governmental police power.
   (b) Any law, ordinance or governmental regulation relating to environmental protection.
   (c) Any law, ordinance or governmental regulation (including but not limited to building and zoning ordinances) restricting or regulating or prohibiting the occupancy, use or enjoyment of the land, or regulating the character, dimensions or location of any improvement now or hereafter erected on the land, or prohibiting a separation in ownership or a change in the dimensions or area of the land or any parcel of which the land is or was a part.
   (d) The effect of any violation of the matters excluded under (a), (b) or (c) above, unless notice of a defect, lien or encumbrance resulting from a violation has been recorded at Date of Policy in those records in which under state statutes deeds, mortgages, lis pendens, liens or other title encumbrances must be recorded in order to impart constructive notice to purchasers of the land for value and without knowledge; provided, however, that without limitation, such records shall not be construed to include records in any of the offices of federal, state or local environmental protection, zoning, building, health or public safety authorities.
2. Rights of eminent domain unless notice of the exercise of such rights appears in the public records at Date of Policy.
3. Defects, liens, encumbrances, adverse claims, or other matters (a) created, suffered, assumed or agreed to by the insured claimant; (b) not known to the Company and not shown by the public records but known to the insured claimant either at Date of Policy or at the date such claimant acquired an estate or interest insured by this policy and not disclosed in writing by the insured claimant to the Company prior to the date such insured claimant became an insured hereunder; (c) resulting in no loss or damage to the insured claimant; (d) attaching or created subsequent to Date of Policy; (e) resulting in loss or damage which would not have been sustained if the insured claimant had paid value for the estate or interest insured by this policy.

CONDITIONS AND STIPULATIONS

1. DEFINITION OF TERMS

The following terms when used in this policy mean:

(a) "insured": the insured named in Schedule A, and, subject to any rights or defenses the Company may have had against the named insured, those who succeed to the interest of such insured by operation of law as distinguished from purchase including, but not limited to, heirs, distributees, devisees, survivors, personal representatives, next of kin, or corporate or fiduciary successors.

(b) "insured claimant": an insured claiming loss or damage hereunder.

(c) "knowledge": actual knowledge, not constructive knowledge or notice which may be imputed to an insured by reason of any public records.

(d) "land": the land described, specifically or by reference in Schedule A, and improvements affixed thereto which by law constitute real property; provided, however, the term "land" does not include any property beyond the lines of the area specifically described or referred to in Schedule A, nor any right, title, interest, estate or easement in abutting streets, roads, avenues, alleys, lanes, ways or waterways, but nothing herein shall modify or limit the extent to which a right of access to and from the land is insured by this policy.

(e) "mortgage": mortgage, deed of trust, trust deed, or other security instrument.

(f) "public records": those records which by law impart constructive notice of matters relating to said land.

2. CONTINUATION OF INSURANCE AFTER CONVEYANCE OF TITLE

The coverage of this policy shall continue in force as of Date of Policy in favor of an insured so long as such insured retains an estate or interest in the land, or holds an indebtedness secured by a purchase money mortgage given by a purchaser from such insured, or so long as such insured shall have liability by reason of covenants of warranty made by such insured in any transfer or conveyance of such estate or interest; provided, however, this policy shall not continue in force in favor of any purchaser from such insured of either said estate or interest or the indebtedness secured by a purchase money mortgage given to such insured.

3. DEFENSE AND PROSECUTION OF ACTIONS – NOTICE OF CLAIM TO BE GIVEN BY AN INSURED CLAIMANT

(a) The Company, at its own cost and without undue delay, shall provide for the defense of an insured in all litigation consisting of actions or proceedings commenced against such insured, or a defense interposed against an insured in an action to enforce a contract for a sale of the estate or interest in said land, to the extent that such litigation is founded upon an alleged defect, lien, encumbrance, or other matter insured against by this policy.

(b) The insured shall notify the Company promptly in writing (i) in case any action or proceeding is begun or defense is interposed as set forth in (a) above, (ii) in case knowledge shall come to an insured hereunder of any claim of title or interest which is adverse to the title to the estate or interest, as insured, and which might cause loss or damage for which the Company may be liable by virtue of this policy, or (iii) if title to the estate or interest, as insured, is rejected as unmarketable. If such prompt notice shall not be given to the Company, then as to such insured all liability of the Company shall cease and terminate in regard to the matter or matters for which such prompt notice is required; provided, however, that failure to notify shall in no case prejudice the rights of any such insured under this policy unless the Company shall be prejudiced by such failure and then only to the extent of such prejudice.

(c) The Company shall have the right at its own cost to institute and without undue delay prosecute any action or proceeding or to do any other act which in its opinion may be necessary or desirable to establish the title to the estate or interest as insured, and the Company may take any appropriate action under the terms of this policy, whether or not it shall be liable thereunder, and shall not thereby concede liability or waive any provision of this policy.

(d) Whenever the Company shall have brought any action or interposed a defense as required or permitted by the provisions of this policy, the Company may pursue any such litigation to final determination by a court of competent jurisdiction and expressly reserves the right, in its sole discretion, to appeal from any adverse judgment or order.

(e) In all cases where this policy permits or requires the Company to prosecute or provide for the defense of any action or proceeding, the insured hereunder shall secure to the Company the right to so prosecute or provide defense in such action or proceeding, and all appeals therein, and permit the Company to use, at its option, the name of such insured for such purpose. Whenever requested by the Company, such insured shall give the Company all reasonable aid in any such action or proceeding, in effecting settlement, securing evidence, obtaining witnesses, or prosecuting or defending such action or proceeding, and the Company shall reimburse such insured for any expense so incurred.

4. NOTICE OF LOSS–LIMITATION OF ACTION

In addition to the notices required under paragraph 3(b) of these Conditions and Stipulations, a statement in writing of any loss or damage for which it is claimed the Company is liable under this policy shall be furnished to the Company within 90 days after such loss or damage shall have been determined and no right of action shall accrue to an insured claimant until 30 days after such statement shall have been furnished. Failure to furnish such statement of loss or damage shall terminate any liability of the Company under this policy as to such loss or damage.

5. OPTIONS TO PAY OR OTHERWISE SETTLE CLAIMS

The Company shall have the option to pay or otherwise settle for or in the name of an insured claimant any claim insured against or to terminate all liability and obligations of the Company hereunder by paying or tendering payment of the amount of insurance under this policy together with any costs, attorneys' fees and expenses incurred up to the time of such payment or tender of payment, by the insured claimant and authorized by the Company.

6. DETERMINATION AND PAYMENT OF LOSS

(a) The liability of the Company under this policy shall in no case exceed the least of:

(i) the actual loss of the insured claimant; or

(ii) the amount of insurance stated in Schedule A.

(b) The Company will pay, in addition to any loss insured against by this policy, all costs imposed upon an insured in litigation carried on by the Company for such insured, and all costs, attorneys' fees and expenses in litigation carried on by such insured with the written authorization of the Company.

(c) When liability has been definitely fixed in accordance with the conditions of this policy, the loss or damage shall be payable within 30 days thereafter.

Conditions and Stipulations Continued Inside Cover

CONDITIONS AND STIPULATIONS

(Continued)

7. LIMITATION OF LIABILITY

No claim shall arise or be maintainable under this policy (a) if the Company, after having received notice of an alleged defect, lien or encumbrance insured against hereunder, by litigation or otherwise, removes such defect, lien or encumbrance or establishes the title, as insured, within a reasonable time after receipt of such notice; (b) in the event of litigation until there has been a final determination by a court of competent jurisdiction, and disposition of all appeals therefrom, adverse to the title, as insured, as provided in paragraph 3 hereof; or (c) for liability voluntarily assumed by an insured in settling any claim or suit without prior written consent of the Company.

8. REDUCTION OF LIABILITY

All payments under this policy, except payments made for costs, attorneys' fees and expenses, shall reduce the amount of the insurance pro tanto. No payment shall be made without producing this policy for endorsement of such payment unless the policy be lost or destroyed, in which case proof of such loss or destruction shall be furnished to the satisfaction of the Company.

9. LIABILITY NONCUMULATIVE

It is expressly understood that the amount of insurance under this policy shall be reduced by any amount the Company may pay under any policy insuring either (a) a mortgage shown or referred to in Schedule B hereof which is a lien on the estate or interest covered by this policy, or (b) a mortgage hereafter executed by an insured which is a charge or lien on the estate or interest described or referred to in Schedule A, and the amount so paid shall be deemed a payment under this policy. The Company shall have the option to apply to the payment of any such mortgages any amount that otherwise would be payable hereunder to the insured owner of the estate or interest covered by this policy and the amount so paid shall be deemed a payment under this policy to said insured owner.

10. APPORTIONMENT

If the land described in Schedule A consists of two or more parcels which are not used as a single site, and a loss is established affecting one or more of said parcels but not all, the loss shall be computed and settled on a pro rata basis as if the amount of insurance under this policy was divided pro rata as to the value on Date of Policy of each separate parcel to the whole, exclusive of any improvements made subsequent to Date of Policy,

unless a liability or value has otherwise been agreed upon as to each such parcel by the Company and the insured at the time of the issuance of this policy and shown by an express statement herein or by an endorsement attached hereto.

11. SUBROGATION UPON PAYMENT OR SETTLEMENT

Whenever the Company shall have settled a claim under this policy, all right of subrogation shall vest in the Company unaffected by any act of the insured claimant. The Company shall be subrogated to and be entitled to all rights and remedies which such insured claimant would have had against any person or property in respect to such claim had this policy not been issued, and if requested by the Company, such insured claimant shall transfer to the Company all rights and remedies against any person or property necessary in order to perfect such right of subrogation and shall permit the Company to use the name of such insured claimant in any transaction or litigation involving such rights or remedies. If the payment does not cover the loss of such insured claimant, the Company shall be subrogated to such rights and remedies in the proportion which said payment bears to the amount of said loss. If loss should result from any act of such insured claimant, such act shall not void this policy, but the Company, in that event, shall be required to pay only that part of any losses insured against hereunder which shall exceed the amount, if any, lost to the Company by reason of the impairment of the right of subrogation.

12. LIABILITY LIMITED TO THIS POLICY

This instrument together with all endorsements and other instruments, if any, attached hereto by the Company is the entire policy and contract between the insured and the Company.

Any claim of loss or damage, whether or not based on negligence, and which arises out of the status of the title to the estate or interest covered hereby or any action asserting such claim, shall be restricted to the provisions and conditions and stipulations of this policy.

No amendment of or endorsement to this policy can be made except by writing endorsed hereon or attached hereto signed by either the President, a Vice President, the Secretary, an Assistant Secretary, or validating officer or authorized signatory of the Company.

13. NOTICES, WHERE SENT

All notices required to be given the Company and any statement in writing required to be furnished the Company shall be addressed to Commonwealth Land Title Insurance Company, Eight Penn Center, Philadelphia, Pennsylvania 19103.

Reprinted with permission of Commonwealth Land Title Insurance Company, Rev. 3/30/84.

State	Severalty Individual	Tenancy in Common	Joint Tenancy	Tenancy by the Entirety	Community Property	Trust	Condominium
Alabama	•	•	•			•	•
Alaska	•	•		•		•	•
Arizona	•	•	•		•	•	•
Arkansas	•	•	•	•		•	•
California	•	•	•		•	•	•
Colorado	•	•	•			•	•
Connecticut	•	•	•			•	•
Delaware	•	•	•	•		•	•
District of Columbia	•	•	•	•		•	•
Florida	•	•	•	•		•	•
Georgia	•	•	•			•	•
Hawaii	•	•	•	•		•	•
Idaho	•	•	•	•	•	•	•
Illinois	•	•	•			•	•
Indiana	•	•	•			•	•
Iowa	•	•	•			•	•
Kansas	•	•	•			•	•
Kentucky	•	•	•	•		•	•
Louisiana[1]						•	•
Maine	•	•	•			•	•
Maryland	•	•	•	•		•	•
Massachusetts	•	•	•	•		•	•
Michigan	•	•	•	•		•	•
Minnesota	•	•	•			•	•
Mississippi	•	•	•			•	•
Missouri	•	•	•			•	•
Montana	•	•	•			•	•
Nebraska	•	•	•			•	•
Nevada	•	•	•		•	•	•
New Hampshire	•	•	•			•	•
New Jersey	•	•	•	•		•	•
New Mexico	•	•	•		•	•	•
New York	•	•	•	•		•	•
North Carolina	•	•	•	•		•	•
North Dakota	•	•	•			•	•
Ohio[2]	•	•		•		•	•
Oklahoma	•	•	•	•		•	•
Oregon	•	•	•	•		•	•
Pennsylvania	•	•	•	•		•	•
Rhode Island	•	•	•	•		•	•
South Carolina	•	•	•		•	•	•
South Dakota	•	•	•			•	•
Tennessee	•	•	•	•		•	•
Texas	•	•	•		•	•	•
Utah	•	•	•	•		•	•
Vermont	•	•	•	•		•	•
Virginia	•	•	•	•		•	•
Washington	•	•	•		•	•	•
West Virginia	•	•	•			•	•
Wisconsin[3]	•	•	•			•	•
Wyoming	•	•	•	•		•	•

[1] In Louisiana, real estate can be owned by one person and by two or more persons, but these ownership interests are created by Louisiana statute. There are no estates comparable to those of joint tenancy, tenancy by the entirety, or community property, nor is there any statutory estate giving surviving co-owners the right of survivorship. Two or more persons may be co-owners under indivision, or joint, ownership.
[2] Ohio does not recognize joint tenancy, but permits a special form of survivorship by deed through an instrument commonly called a "joint and survivorship deed."
[3] As of 1986, Wisconsin recognizes "marital property" that is similar to community property.

A.

U.S. DEPARTMENT OF HOUSING & URBAN DEVELOPMENT
SETTLEMENT STATEMENT

B. TYPE OF LOAN:

1. ☐ FHA   2. ☐ FmHA   3. ☐ CONV. UNINS.
4. ☐ VA   5. ☐ CONV. INS.

6. FILE NUMBER: 7. LOAN NUMBER:

8. MORTGAGE INSURANCE CASE NUMBER:

C. NOTE: *This form is furnished to give you a statement of actual settlement costs. Amounts paid to and by the settlement agent are shown. Items marked "(p.o.c.)" were paid outside the closing; they are shown here for informational purposes and are not included in the totals.*

D. NAME AND ADDRESS OF BORROWER:

E. NAME AND ADDRESS OF SELLER:

F. NAME AND ADDRESS OF LENDER:

G. PROPERTY LOCATION:

H. SETTLEMENT AGENT:

PLACE OF SETTLEMENT:

I. SETTLEMENT DATE:

J. SUMMARY OF BORROWER'S TRANSACTION	
100. GROSS AMOUNT DUE FROM BORROWER:	
101. Contract sales price	
102. Personal property	
103. Settlement charges to borrower (line 1400)	
104.	
105.	
Adjustments for items paid by seller in advance	
106. City/town taxes to	
107. County taxes to	
108. Assessments to	
109.	
110.	
111.	
112.	

K. SUMMARY OF SELLER'S TRANSACTION	
400. GROSS AMOUNT DUE TO SELLER:	
401. Contract sales price	
402. Personal property	
403.	
404.	
405.	
Adjustments for items paid by seller in advance	
406. City/town taxes to	
407. County taxes to	
408. Assessments to	
409.	
410.	
411.	
412.	

	GROSS AMOUNT DUE FROM BORROWER	
120.		

200. AMOUNT PAID BY OR IN BEHALF OF BORROWER:

201.	Deposit or earnest money	
202.	Principal amount of new loan(s)	
203.	Existing loan(s) taken subject to	
204.		
205.		
206.		
207		
208.		
209.		

Adjustments for items unpaid by seller

210.	City/town taxes	to	
211.	County taxes	to	
212.	Assessments	to	
213.			
214.			
215.			
216.			
217.			
218.			
219.			
220.	**TOTAL PAID BY/FOR BORROWER**		

300. CASH AT SETTLEMENT FROM/TO BORROWER

301.	Gross amount due from borrower (line 120)	
302.	Less amounts paid by/for borrower (line 220)	( )
303.	**CASH (☐ FROM) (☐ TO) BORROWER**	

	GROSS AMOUNT DUE TO SELLER	
420.		

500. REDUCTIONS IN AMOUNT DUE TO SELLER:

501.	Excess deposit (see instructions)	
502.	Settlement charges to seller (line 1400)	
503.	Existing loan(s) taken subject to	
504.	Payoff of first mortgage loan	
505.	Payoff of second mortgage loan	
506.		
507		
508.		
509.		

Adjustments for items unpaid by seller

510.	City/town taxes	to	
511.	County taxes	to	
512.	Assessments	to	
513.			
514.			
515.			
516.			
517.			
518.			
519.			
520.	**TOTAL REDUCTION AMOUNT DUE SELLER**		

600. CASH AT SETTLEMENT TO/FROM SELLER

601.	Gross amount due to seller (line 420)	
602.	Less reductions in amount due seller (line 520)	( )
603.	**CASH (☐ TO) (☐ FROM) SELLER**	

The undersigned hereby acknowledges receipt of a completed copy of pages 1 and 2 of this statement and any attachments referred to herein.

Borrower _____

Borrower _____

Seller _____

Seller _____

SETTLEMENT STATEMENT

Page 2

L. SETTLEMENT CHARGES

	PAID FROM BORROWER'S FUNDS AT SETTLEMENT	PAID FROM SELLER'S FUNDS AT SETTLEMENT
700. TOTAL SALES/BROKER'S COMMISSION based on price $ @ % =		
Division of Commission (line 700) as follows:		
701. $ to		
702. $ to		
703. Commission paid at Settlement		
704.		
800. ITEMS PAYABLE IN CONNECTION WITH LOAN		
801. Loan Origination Fee %		
802. Loan Discount %		
803. Appraisal Fee to		
804. Credit Report to		
805. Lender's Inspection Fee		
806. Mortgage Insurance Application Fee to		
807. Assumption Fee		
808.		
809.		
810.		
811.		
900. ITEMS REQUIRED BY LENDER TO BE PAID IN ADVANCE		
901. Interest from to @ $ /day		
902. Mortgage Insurance Premium for months to		
903. Hazard Insurance Premium for years to		
904. years to		
905.		
1000. RESERVES DEPOSITED WITH LENDER		
1001. Hazard Insurance months @ $ per month		
1002. Mortgage Insurance months @ $ per month		
1003. City Property Taxes months @ $ per month		
1004. County Property Taxes months @ $ per month		
1005. Annual Assessments months @ $ per month		
1006. months @ $ per month		
1007. months @ $ per month		
1008. months @ $ per month		

1100. TITLE CHARGES

1101. Settlement or closing fee	to			
1102. Abstract or title search	to			
1103. Title Examination	to			
1104. Title Insurance binder	to			
1105. Document preparation	to			
1106. Notary fees	to			
1107. Attorney's fees	to			
(includes above items numbers:		)		
1108. Title insurance	to			
(includes above items numbers:		)		
1109. Lender's coverage	$			
1110. Owner's coverage	$			
1111.				
1112.				
1113.				

1200. GOVERNMENT RECORDING AND TRANSFER CHARGES

1201. Recording fees: Deed $	; Mortgage $	; Releases $	
1202. City/county tax/stamps: Deed $	; Mortgage $		
1203. State tax/stamps: Deed $	; Mortgage $		
1204.			
1205.			

1300. ADDITIONAL SETTLEMENT CHARGES

1301. Survey	to	
1302. Pest inspection	to	
1303.		
1304.		
1305.		

1400. TOTAL SETTLEMENT CHARGES (enter on lines 103, Section J and 502, Section K)

By signing Page 1 of this statement, the signatories of Page 1 also acknowledge receipt of a completed copy of Page 2 of this two page statement.

Fee Simple Deed

This Indenture Made this   day of   19

Between

(hereinafter called the Grantor   ),

(hereinafter called the Grantee   ),

Witnesseth   That the said Grantor   for and in consideration of the sum of

lawful money of the United States of America, unto   well and truly paid by the said Grantee   , at or before the sealing and delivery hereof, the receipt whereof is hereby acknowledged,   granted, bargained and sold, released and confirmed, and by these presents   grant, bargain and sell, release and confirm unto the said Grantee   ,   and assigns,

Together with all and singular the   improvements, ways, streets, alleys, driveways, passages, waters, water-courses, rights, liberties, privileges, hereditaments and appurtenances, whatsoever unto the hereby granted premises belonging, or in any wise appertaining, and the reversions and remainders, rents, issues, and profits thereof; and all the estate, right, title, interest, property, claim and demand whatsoever of the said Grantor   , as well at law as in equity, of, in, and to the same.

To have and to hold the said lot   or piece   of ground above described with the   hereditaments and premises hereby granted, or mentioned, and intended so to be, with the appurtenances, unto the said Grantee   , and assigns, to and for the only proper use and behoof of the said Grantee   ,   and assigns forever.

And the said Grantor   , for

do   , by these presents, covenant, grant and agree, to and with the said Grantee   ,   and assigns, that   the said Grantor   , all and singular the hereditaments and premises herein above described and granted, or mentioned and intended so to be, with the appurtenances, unto the said Grantee   ,   and assigns, against   , the said Grantor   ,   and against all and every person or persons whomsoever lawfully claiming or to claim the same or any part thereof, by, from or under or any of them shall and will   WARRANT and forever DEFEND.

In Witness Whereof, The said Grantor   has   caused these presents to be duly executed the day and year first herein above written.

Sealed and Delivered
IN THE PRESENCE OF US:

COMMONWEALTH OF PENNSYLVANIA
COUNTY OF   On this, the   day of   19   ,
                                                  before me, the undersigned officer, personally appeared

(IND.)   known to me (or satisfactorily proven) to be the person ,   whose name   subscribed to
                the within instrument, and acknowledged that   he   executed the same for the purposes therein
                contained.

    or

                who acknowledged himself to be the   of
(CORP.)   , a corporation, and that he as such
                being authorized to do so, executed the foregoing instrument for the purpose therein contained by
                signing the name of the corporation by himself as

                𝕴𝖓 𝖂𝖎𝖙𝖓𝖊𝖘𝖘 𝖂𝖍𝖊𝖗𝖊𝖔𝖋,   I hereunto set my hand and official seal.

                                                  ....NOTARY PUBLIC

— 13 —
Single Buyers Speak Out

Single buyers are an ever-growing part of the real estate marketplace. Some single buyers are first-time home buyers, some are single again and have previously owned a house with a spouse, some are single parents, still others are buying for the second or third time as they move up in the world. Whichever category you fall into, you are part of a large number of active real estate consumers.

You should be well informed when you buy a house. Only you know what will suit your needs. Only you can protect yourself from making unnecessary mistakes when buying real estate. Only you can do your homework! Ask questions. Ask lots of questions!

The commentaries included here are for your information. Each of the people you will read about are happy homeowners now and hope that their experiences can be helpful to other single buyers. Each has agreed to share his or her story with you so that you will enjoy the experience of homeownership as a single person as they do. Some of these people are single, some are single again, and all of them know firsthand the trials and tribulations of buying a home.

SCOTT, SMALL BUSINESS OWNER

It was not the first home that I had bought as a single person, but it was the most difficult without a doubt. I had always been employed by a reputable, large business before being self-employed as a business owner. I was unprepared for the difficult time I would have securing financing for the house I wanted to buy.

The first problem was that I had only been in business for three years when I decided to buy another house. The financing company wanted a five-year business history, I only had three, the first three. I had a business partner, which they saw as a potential liability. The lender insisted that I pay off my car loan and sell my current residence before settlement on the house that I wanted to buy. They required that I justify all and any gifts from friends or family being put toward payment. Case in point: I needed a note from my mother declaring the money she had given to me to be a gift, not a loan. (Author's Note: This is a very common requirement of lenders.)

If I had not been determined to buy the house of my dreams, this ordeal would have defeated me early in the application process. I believe that it worked out because my Realtor, a long-time colleague, went to bat for me with his friend at the financing company. My family provided additional financial assistance to help meet the demands of the financing company. I had made up my mind that this was an excellent buy and worth the battle. I was right! The Realtor helped me sell my house and buy the big stone Colonial I had long dreamed of owning. It took a team effort, but in the end, the requirements set by the lending company were met to their satisfaction and settlement on the property was scheduled. I was thrilled. The day of settlement arrived and although we squabbled over a rain gutter for awhile, my lawyer was able to work this detail out and we completed the settlement. I now have a delightful home that was well worth all the trouble it took to own it.

DAVID, VIET NAM VETERAN

War is a terrible thing. It causes family stress and sometimes even separation. In my case, it changed my life. I was a young man when I went to war. When I came home, my wife left me. I came home from work one day to an empty house. She took the furniture, the bank account, and the wedding gifts. I found out through her lawyer that she wanted a divorce. I had to sell the house to make the settlement demands.

I lived for a time in an apartment, but I was used to owning a house. I had a good job. I felt dissatisfied, however, because the company was changing. They wanted me to move, and I really wanted to stay on the West Coast. They agreed to let me stay. I am a veteran and I have been a stable employee.

I am currently renting the house I am buying. During this year, my rent is going toward closing costs. I have agreed to the price and have until my lease ends this year to get a mortgage. I am getting a VA loan. My advice to readers is to build a good credit history, have stable employment, and minimize debt before you go for a mortgage.

BERNIE, SELF-EMPLOYED HAIR STYLIST

I found just the building I wanted to live in and have my business in, too. It was in the Historic District of the city, right near other businesses and government offices. It would need to be renovated to suit my plans and that is where my story could be

your story! I hope that I can help you avoid some of the setbacks by sharing what happened to me.

I found out that I would need to see a city code inspection report on the house I wanted to buy so that I would be aware of the violations that needed to be fixed either by me or the seller. I also was told that I would need a permit from the city to work on the violations. Because the house was in the Historic District, I would also need to talk with the Historic District Review Board regarding my plans. It all seemed easy enough, so I applied for the permit and talked with the board. But you know the old story, if you don't know what the questions are, you can't ask them! It became clear to me that many different permits were needed; some for interior work, some for exterior work, one for electric, and one for plumbing. In addition to this, permits can only be applied for at specified dates in any particular month.

Once I applied for the permit and the Board reviewed it, I was asked to appear before the Board with my architectural drawings and color samples. Three months had passed by this time. I finally asked the city for some guidelines. There were none. The position they took was that if I had asked the questions first, I would not have had these problems! My advice to you is to talk with someone who has had similar work done and gather as many questions as you can.

JANE, YOUNG COLLEGE PROFESSOR

My advice is to rally as many friends and associates as you can to help you ask all the questions you need answered. The Realtor will be representing the seller, so you will need to have some help. I realized that although things like the school district, number of bedrooms, number of bathrooms, amount of storage, and location of parks and stores were moderately important to me as a single person, these factors are of utmost importance to me if I plan to sell my house in the future to a family. I decided to get these features in the house I bought as a future investment for my property. I found that what I thought was too big for me was indeed the space I needed. So don't shortchange yourself.

LORRAINE, ELEMENTARY SCHOOL TEACHER

When I first contemplated buying a home, I was single and had been teaching school for ten years. I had very little money in the bank. I was living quite happily in a little trailer in the country on five acres of rented land.

A friend of mine began encouraging me to buy property. It was pointed out to me that while I was blissful in my single stage in the country, I was not investing my money anywhere and owned no property. I had a friend who was involved in real estate and owned a property in a changing neighborhood in the city that she suggested I buy from her. After some basic work that it needed, she said I would be able to sell the property at a profit and afford the home of my dreams. I was convinced, though reluctant, to leave my spot in the country. I knew I was a novice and told my friend that I would need help in putting this deal together, for I knew nothing about real estate. My friend promised to walk me through the loan application process and spend some time helping me renovate the property for the first three months on weekends.

She held true to her word. She went to the bank with me for a loan and when closing day arrived, picked me up and drove me to the bank. The only problem that arose was when the bank officer asked me for proof of homeowner's insurance. I had no idea that I needed to buy insurance *before* I bought the house. So off I went to my insurance agent to purchase a homeowner's policy. Proof in hand, we returned that day to the bank to complete the settlement and finalize the closing.

I moved into the house that month and did some remodeling on it for the next four years. I sold it for twice what I paid for it and moved to a neighborhood more to my taste. It was an exciting experience. What I am most grateful for is the opportunity to have had an affordable start that allowed me to step up to the wonderful home I now live in.

MARGY, PSYCHOTHERAPIST

The first house I ever made an offer on was a close call with disaster. I was looking for something that would make a good investment eventually as a rental property. I thought that I would live in it for awhile and then take in a tenant. I came upon a house with two units that was in a good neighborhood and was modestly priced. I thought this would be better because I could live in one unit and rent the other. After going through the house with a Realtor, it seemed like just the right place. The floors were nicely carpeted, and the walls were all paneled to look fresh and new. I made an offer and put down a deposit.

I went for a cup of coffee to celebrate my initiation into property ownership. As I sat there going over the house in my mind, I began to have a vague sense of uneasiness. Was it the tin roof that had no insulation? Perhaps the railroad track that lay just a few feet from the lovely garden in the backyard? What structural problems could all that paneling and carpet be hiding? I ran to my car and drove back to the neighborhood.

As I circled the block, nervously looking at the house for reassurance, I spotted a neighbor mowing his lawn. I rolled down my window and shouted, "Excuse me, but do you know anything about the house over there?" "Well," he said, "I wouldn't touch it with a ten foot pole! You couldn't pay me to buy it!" He continued to confirm my worst nightmares about some very expensive problems with the house. That one question saved me thousands of dollars!

I quickly contacted the Realtor to withdraw my offer. Luckily, he had not yet extended my offer to the owner, and although he was not obliged to do so, he was kind enough to destroy the offer and return my deposit.

Since then, I have learned many lessons, and now I own a three-bedroom house in a great neighborhood.

JUDY, MIDDLE SCHOOL TEACHER

The thought of being on my own was all at once exhilarating and frightening. Being single all my life, but always involved with someone to share financial responsibilities, I was for the first time in my life at the age of forty-five facing life solo. My last relationship of fourteen years had drained me financially as I put most of my earnings into someone else's property and business. I was faced with little money in my checking account and even less in my savings account. However, I had been teaching for twenty-four years and had established excellent credit. My greatest asset was a personal belief in myself that I could do what I needed and wanted to do and a willingness to plunge ahead. I decided to buy a house after a great deal of soul searching.

Being a complete novice, I enlisted the help of a local real estate agency. I quickly discovered that the agencies in my area represent the seller. After a few rocky relationships with local agencies, and lots of my own dogged searching and driving about, I went to an open house and discovered an agent I liked. We "clicked" and together searched for my home. By this time, I knew just what I wanted — the location and the price I was willing to pay. In fact, I had even located a little house on the river, with a For Sale By Owner sign on it. I decided to work all of this through the Realtor rather than going directly to the owner as some might do. I felt better working with someone with the necessary expertise to guide me through this purchase. As it happened, the agent listed the house and sold it to me as we had agreed.

Financing was the next step. I found out that first-time home buyers in my area have a lot of options, especially someone like myself who does not earn a lot of money. My Realtor helped me choose the lending institution and also mentioned the Bond Money Program in our state available for first-time home buyers who make under $37,000 (this qualifying income can change several times a year). Interest rates are usually a whole percentage point below those of conventional mortgages and only 5% down payment is required. To apply for this, I went to a participating bank, filled out tons of government forms, and was interviewed by the local bank's loan officer. My name was entered into a lottery drawing with the state. My name was drawn and I received the Bond money!

As with most government policies and regulations, there were stringent rules regarding what was needed for closing. Inspections were carried out on the flooring and its covering, septic and well water systems, and details of the insurance policy. It was made clear to me that the property could not be rented and was to be my principal residence for nine years, or penalties could be invoked.

QUICK CHECKLIST
SINGLE BUYERS SPEAK OUT

1. Be sure you can satisfy the conditions set forth by the Lender.
2. Be sure that you are a good credit risk.
3. Be sure to check any requirements of the local government for Historic District Restoration permits.
4. Take friends along with you to see the properties you like and ask their opinions.
5. Ask people who have experience in buying a house as many questions as you can think of as you learn the ropes.
6. Find a professional Realtor to work with when the time comes, if you wish.
7. Ask your lawyer to come to settlement with you.
8. Beware of the "white elephant" property. Remember: You will probably want to sell it someday!
9. Talk with the neighbors about the house you want to buy.
10. Remember, you may be able to buy a place that needs some work but will pay off for you later when you sell it and move to a nicer home.

— 14 —
Buying with Another Person

Like many business transactions, buying a property with another person is a legal and binding contract and a major investment. It should be thought through very carefully. Joe and William decided to buy a house together after they graduated from college. They were brothers who trusted each other, knew each other well, and were good friends. They took title as Tenants in Common, which they knew their parents, living in a nearby town, had done. Only after Joe, who had no will, was killed in an automobile accident did the issue of Joe's share of the property come into question. What should Joe and William have done to secure the property's ownership in the case of either of their untimely deaths?

If Joe had intended that William become the sole owner of the house, he should have said so in a will and they should have taken title as Tenants in Common with Right of Survivorship. Joe and William took title as Tenants in Common, which meant that when Joe died, his share of the house passed on to his family. In this case, his mother and father inherited Joe's share of their children's house. Imagine how complicated this can become among unrelated single owners!

This chapter presents an alternative to buying a home alone. What should you know about buying a property with someone else? What are the potential pitfalls? Do the lenders prefer two buyers to one? Does it make it easier to buy and maintain a house if there is more than one buyer? Before you venture into a contract as significant as buying a house with another person, be sure to do your homework! It is also important to have a will.

SHARING OWNERSHIP

You may have decided that you would like to buy a house with another person. The reasons vary widely for this decision. Clearly two incomes make a house more affordable. It is important that both owners are wage earners. The total responsibility of home ownership can be shared. The cost of repairs, utilities, taxes, emergency repairs, and other expenses will be divided equitably. Each person will have a bit more cash flow for his or her own needs.

On the surface, this seems like a good idea. It sounds like a partnership. Indeed, it is just that — a partnership. It is a legally binding contract between the owners. Each owner is equally responsible and can be held legally accountable.

It is important that the people who are about to enter into a property partnership set down the ground rules they intend to follow. The following questions should be discussed and answered:

1. Will the ownership be 50/50, or will one of the partners own a larger share based on the amount of money contributed to the purchase?

2. If in the future one of the owners wants to sell, how will this be handled? Will the remaining owner have the first right of refusal to buy out

the other owner? Will you set a buyout formula for the partner so that it is affordable? Will you restrict family members from buying in? Will the move of one of the partners break the contract and force a sale? How can you protect your investment?

3. How will you deed the property when you buy it? What will happen to the property if one of the partners should die? This can be protected in the deed as well as in a will. If this is important to you and your investment, consider this very carefully. Remember that Tenancy in Common is very different from Tenancy in Common with Right of Survivorship. Decide which option you want to use to take title to the property:

   Tenancy in Common. Each owner holds an undivided interest in the entire property, which does not terminate upon death but passes to the relatives of the deceased unless directed otherwise in a will.

   Tenancy in Common with Right of Survivorship. Owners must have one and the same interest, which accrues at the same conveyance and begins at the same time. Upon death of one joint tenant, the entire interest in the property passes to the surviving tenant(s).

   Tenancy by the Entirety. This form of ownership is usually by husband and wife, wherein each owns the entire property. In the event of the death of one party, the survivor owns the property without probate.

   Grantee and His/Her Heirs. This form of ownership is often used with single buyers. It is much like Tenancy in Common.

4. What agreements have you worked out regarding guests in the house? How about long-term visitors? What if one of the parties gets married? Get this worked out before you buy into the partnership.

5. Who is going to be responsible for the bookkeeping — paying the bills, arranging for repairs, groceries, and general upkeep?

6. How do you want to record your agreements on these issues? Will it be reviewed and discussed periodically? Should it be formalized like a business contract with your lawyer?

Remember that the issues must be settled *before* the partnership is in place. After you have signed all the paperwork that goes along with buying a property it is generally too late to establish the way you want the partnership to work. Even if it is not too late, it is certainly much more difficult.

POTENTIAL PITFALLS

The first words out of a pair of prospective single home buyers regarding these issues is usually, "Oh, we don't have to worry about those things, we know what we are doing." If so, then the following pitfalls will not be of any concern to you. On the other hand, consider the following "red flags":

- After buying the house, your partner loses his/her job. Will the financial situation put you at risk? Have you both agreed how to work this out ahead of time?

- After moving into the house, you discover that your new co-owner has plans to do some major renovations. Have you discussed how this decision was made? Who is responsible for all the costs? Is it going to enhance the value of the property or devalue it? If you disagree, what are the procedures you have established for settling disputes of this magnitude?

- After living in the house for a few months, your co-owner decides to buy a pet. Has this been discussed thoroughly? What are the ground rules for pet behavior in the house if you both agree to the newcomer? If a major disagreement follows, how have you decided to negotiate the solution?

- Your partner decides to get married. Did you work out the details of a buyout in advance of buying the property?

- Your partner brings a friend into the house to live with him/her. Are there clear house rules for this situation?

LENDERS' PREFERENCES

Lenders want low risk buyers, whether they are single or not. They are not in the business of lending money to lose it. They set up stringent guidelines for the borrower. If each buyer has a good job with a steady income and a stable employment history with low debt, chances are very good that a lender will qualify them for the house they want to buy. The lender may look at each buyer as though they would have the debt alone. On the other hand, with two sources of income, the chances are you will look stronger to the lender than if you were applying alone with a modest income.

DOWN PAYMENT

There is a Catch-22 here. Generally, the more money each of you puts into the purchase, the less you need to borrow, and the more likely you will qualify for the loan. On the other hand, it is always a good idea to use as little of your own savings and as much of the lender's money as possible when making a large purchase. What should you do? This is a tricky situation. The less your monthly payment, the better your ultimate cash flow. With two or more owners, the home may be easily affordable. Get advice from your accountant on this issue. Every combination of buyers is unique. There is no one answer here.

WHEN TWO BUY AND MAINTAIN A HOUSE

It may be easier for each co-owner to share the cost of the house and its maintenance than to do it alone. This is true as long as both owners continue to earn an income, have interest in the house, and see it as an investment to protect. The more cooperation there is in the long-term care of a property, the better it is for the property value over time. If the burden falls to one or the other person after the expectation was to share the upkeep, chances are, the property and the friendship will suffer. This is an important aspect of co-ownership and should be thoroughly discussed before purchasing a house together.

TITLE

The question of title was discussed in Chapter 12, but it is too important to take lightly when the question of home ownership is involved. Remember that the deed/title to your home is a legal document and spells out who owns the home and how the ownership passes to another in the case of death or divorce. Be sure that you understand the choices. Talk with your lawyer, and remember that you have some choices.

Gretchen and her friend Mary bought a farmhouse in need of work on three acres. The division of labor was fairly equal until Mary moved out to live with her boyfriend. Gretchen wanted to keep the house, but she was unable to do all the work alone and did not want renters. The pair finally sold the house and divided the small profit.

Phil and Mark loved the old brownstone. It needed work. Phil was a photographer. Mark was a lawyer and a good carpenter. Together they renovated the three stories, with an office on the first floor for Mark and a darkroom on the second floor for Phil. There was plenty of room for living space for both men, and they enjoyed having large parties. When Tom decided to marry and buy another home with his wife, Phil wanted to stay in the brownstone. They kept joint ownership. Tom kept his office there and paid Phil a maintenance fee for general upkeep.

YOUR WILL

In most states, your property will pass to your blood relatives after your death. If you wish your property to go to someone other than family, you can make your wishes known with a will.

A valid will should be typed or printed. (Handwritten wills are not valid in all states.) It should state that it is your will, and it must be signed and dated by the will writer, who must have two to three witnesses at the time of the signing. The witnesses are people who will not receive anything under the will. They sign after the will writer.

Be aware that Louisiana law is based on French Law and functions differently than laws in other states.

Most states will recognize a will as valid when the following parts are included:

- Your full name and address.

- A revocation declaring this to be the most current and valid will, voiding any and all that went before it.

- Provisions for the needs of your heirs; custody or trusts for minor children.

- Named beneficiaries for personal property and money.

- Named beneficiaries for real estate.

- Other gifts to people or organizations.

- Name of your executor or executrix — someone you trust and can rely on to carry out the wishes of your will. You will need to state that the executor or executrix will "serve without Bond" or "My executor is specifically relieved from the duty or obligation of filling any Bond or Bonds."

- Funeral and burial arrangements should be specified as you wish.

- Signatures and witnesses with a date.

It is very important that you discuss these items with your lawyer. As a single person, you must provide for the distribution of your estate in the event of an untimely death.

If you give copies of your will to people other than your lawyer, do not sign the copies. This will avoid later confusion of a duplicate will, especially if you have subsequently changed your will.

QUICK CHECKLIST
BUYING A HOUSE WITH ANOTHER PERSON

1. Buying a property with another person is a business transaction and should be carefully and legally agreed upon.
2. Do you know the motives/plans of the other buyer?
3. Have you considered the legal steps to buy out the partner?
4. How have you structured the percentage of ownership?
5. How will the deed be titled regarding ownership in the case of death? Is your will current?
6. Have you considered the potential pitfalls?
7. Can you afford the house alone?
8. How have you decided to share the cost of maintenance?
9. Are you willing to take this financial risk?
10. How well do you know your partner in this transaction?

— 15 —
Handyman's Special

Steve had always wanted to fix up a house of his own. He was ready to leave his parent's home and buy his own house. He had saved his money and knew the community where he would like to live. It was the town he had grown up in and knew very well. An elderly couple in town had recently put their house up for sale. They had made plans to move to a retirement community in a few months. Steve knew that although the house was well maintained during the fifty-five years the couple lived there, it was not modern enough for him. He decided that he would fix it up to suit himself after he bought it. Steve bought the house in January. He moved in immediately and soon realized that living in the house while renovating it was going to take far longer and cost far more than he had ever anticipated. Did Steve have any alternatives to make this project easier and less costly?

Steve could have stayed at home with his parents a bit longer while he worked on his "fixer-upper" house. He would have been able to get major projects like painting, plastering, woodworking, floors, and so on done, without the problem of personal belongings in the way.

Many people are very handy and thoroughly enjoy fixing up old rundown properties. If you are in that category, you might consider this option when looking for your house. There are several very important considerations if you choose to venture into this kind of purchase.

If you are considering buying a "fixer-upper" property, it is critical that you have the property in-spected by a professional building inspector before final ratification of the purchase contract. The property may look as though it needs only superficial, cosmetic work: paint, wallpaper, new vinyl floor, etc. You may not be able to tell that the roof has leaked, or the water heater is about to give up, or the main beam is sagging without help from an expert.

WHO WILL DO THE WORK?

You will have to consider who will be doing the actual repair and restoration work if you buy a rundown property. The more you can do, the better. If you have friends who can help, that is another plus. If you know reliable craftsmen with reasonable rates, you will be able to keep costs down to a minimum.

Plumbing

In many places, a licensed plumber is required to work on plumbing repairs or major plumbing projects in the house. But even if you are able to do this work on your own, be prepared for the job to take longer and cost more than you anticipated. This is especially true in older houses. A simple job like putting in a new kitchen can bring surprises: old walls crumbling before your very eyes, old pipes breaking off, pinhole leaks, odd sizes to fit, and rotten floorboards under appliances. No matter who does the work, a building permit is usually needed to begin the renovation. Allow enough time, money, and skills to get the job done.

Electrical System

As with plumbing, many places require a licensed electrician to work on electrical projects in a home. Electric service to a house is important, and great care must be used when working with it. Old houses frequently have old knob and tube wiring throughout the house. This is usually inadequate for today's home electrical needs. Usually you will want to have at least 100 amp service and sometimes more. No one wants to experience an electrical fire. If you intend to upgrade the electrical service in the house, work with an experienced electrician.

Heating and Cooling Systems

You are likely to find that the old house you bought still has the original furnace. Heating is another service in the home that is very important, and you should be well informed before you tackle this system. In old houses, coal-fired furnaces were often used along with radiant heat (warm air rising through open grates on the floors above the basement and first floor). If this is the type of heating the house has, you will not have ductwork or radiators in the house.

Most heating systems rely on air or water being pumped throughout the house in ducts or pipework from the heating source. The energy source for this can be oil, gas, electricity, solar energy, radiant heat, wood, or coal. If the house is only in need of a new boiler for the furnace, this can be affordable. This is referred to as a conversion boiler. If the house has access to gas, you may be able to convert from oil or coal. If the property is well insulated, you might consider an electric heat pump system. Whatever you decide, consult with experienced specialists. It is a good idea to study this question very carefully before you decide what would be best for the situation. Conversion could be nearly as expensive as a new furnace and far less efficient.

Air conditioning also requires special training and experience. Some houses are easier to work on than others. If, for example, the house has a hot air heating system with ductwork, central air conditioning is relatively easy to install onto the existing system. If the heating system is water or steam, installing air conditioning is a far more expensive and complicated task. Costs are generally high for this renovation. Once again, check with the experts for details. Consider the amount of insulation your old house has. Without good insulation and what we could call a "tight" house, air conditioning may cost you a whole lot more than you imagined.

Roofing

If the old house needs a new roof, be sure you have the skill and tools needed for such a major task. You will have to know how to protect the inside of the house from water damage in the event of rain while you are replacing the roof. You will have to know how to get rid of the debris, and you will need a building permit. Talk with subcontractors for this one. Remember your liability if you have helpers. Working on a roof is dangerous, and you will have to be very careful and skilled.

Flooring

This may be a manageable project. You will need to know if the subflooring is in need of replacement or repair or in good condition before you can proceed with other flooring projects. Usually you will be considering carpeting, tile, vinyl, and wood restoration and sealants. Measuring is the key to this project. How much surface do you want to cover and with what? How is the product packaged? What tools are needed to complete the job? Talk with reputable suppliers before you decide to do a flooring job yourself.

Windows

The question you will need to answer is, what kind of windows are needed and how many? If you are only concerned with adding triple track storm and screen windows, for example, your job need not be difficult or expensive. You will have to measure each window and order the sizes you need. If you have the ladder, tools, and caulk needed, it is possible to do this project on your own.

If you are planning to replace the old windows, you will again have to measure and order the windows you want to replace. Make sure that you have the tools necessary to remove the old windows and to install the replacement windows. This can be an expensive job, and you will certainly need a helper as replacement windows are heavy.

Doors

Generally, this job is done with relatively little trouble. However, in old houses be prepared for warped door jambs, rotten frames, and odd-sized openings. Be prepared to do the carpentry that may be needed to make this job a success. Once again, measure what you need, order the door you want, and be sure to have the tools needed to install it.

Carpentry

Everywhere you look in an old house in need of renovations, you will see the need to have carpentry skills. Take some courses and learn all that you can before you tackle old house renovations. This can be a most rewarding part of renovating your house.

Masonry

Masonry is a skill that is fast disappearing. If this is an area in which you shine, you will be able to do wonders for your old house. Projects both inside and out can be well worth the time and energy. Be sure that you have the proper equipment for any project in this category. Wear a dust mask if you decide to get into taking down an old horsehair plaster wall or work on fancy plastering on wallboard.

Landscaping

This can be the final touches on your old house. A few well-placed plants, shrubs, trees, walkways, and outdoor light fixtures can make a big difference to both the look of your house and its security. You can usually do this with the help of a nearby nursery. They will often have free advice for you in addition to some good buys and healthy specimens for your home.

Insulation

Old houses are frequently short on insulation, so you will have to check this out. If the house has an attic, you will be able to roll batt insulation on the floor to help insulate the house. The walls of the house may be a bit more difficult. You should consult a company that can help you identify where the most heat loss is coming from in your house. Usually the electric or gas companies will provide this service at no cost. That will help you decide what to do about the problems you discover.

Painting

Exterior painting of siding or trim can be tackled with the right ladders and equipment. Have friends over to help. Get good paint, prepare the surface as recommended, attend to details, and count on several days of good weather for this project.

Interior painting is another project that can be done with friends. Trim and detail work needs to be done by someone who prefers such work. Windows and doors are in that category. Walls and ceilings are for the generalists in the group. Be sure to protect the floors. It is always a good idea to paint before you work on the floors. Remember that what you do not paint or finish before you move in probably will not be finished for some time. So try to complete this task before you move your furniture into the house.

Wall Covering

When you begin this task, be sure you have carefully measured the area that you intend to cover. If you run short of the paper you have selected, you may not be able to get a matching dye lot of the needed paper. As you look at wallpaper, keep in mind that some paper is much easier to work with than others. If you are a novice, look for pre-pasted double rolls. (European double rolls measure differently from American double rolls.) This project will need a ladder, a sharp knife, a water tray especially made for wallpaper rolls, paste if your paper is not pre-pasted, and a plumb line to start your wallpaper on a straight line. Why not start out with a small bathroom for practice?

Permits

In many locations it is necessary to secure a permit to do any major repairs or remodeling. Licensed craftsmen are required in most locations to do electrical, plumbing, and masonry work. If you fail to secure a permit, you can be fined or required to undo what you have done. It is very important that you ask the local government office what their requirements are for fixing up a rundown property. Then follow the local regulations. If the property is in a historic district or is designated as a historic property, you will be required to follow stringent rules for the appearance of your property. Be sure to check out these special requirements or restrictions before you contract for the services or do the services yourself.

FINDING A CONTRACTOR

If you decide you simply don't want to tackle major projects yourself, you will need to hire a contractor. Don't just look in the yellow pages and hire the first name you come across. The advice of friends and colleagues is a great place to start. Ask any contractor for several references from satisfied customers.

It is always wise to have a written contract for the work you will have done. Never pay a contractor for the entire job up-front. He or she will definitely require a deposit before beginning the work, but it should be no more than one-third or one-half of the contracted sum. You may want to consider withholding a portion of the final payment until you have determined that the work was done properly. For instance, if you have a new roof put on, it might make sense to wait for the first big rainstorm before handing over final payment. This ensures the contractor will come back to do any repair work necessary.

GOOD ADVICE

Try to complete one room at a time, especially if you are living in the house as you work. It will give you a sense of accomplishment to finish each room and provide an orderly, clean place to rest when your chores are done for the day.

Remember that you can take a course or two at the local community college or vocational/technical center in home improvements and repairs. Even if you feel that you will find contractors to help with this enterprise, it is extremely helpful to have some knowledge of your own.

QUICK CHECKLIST HANDYMAN'S SPECIAL

1. Who will fix all of the problems?
2. What will it cost?
3. How will costs be divided up if you own with other owners?
4. How long will it take to make the house livable?
5. Should professional contractors be hired?
6. How much can you do yourself?
7. Will you build these costs into your mortgage or keep them in a separate home improvement or construction loan?
8. Is the property sound enough to make this a worthwhile project?
9. Will you need special permits and approvals from the local regulatory boards, commissioners, or councils?
10. Will you live in the property while you renovate or fix it up?

— 16 —
Features that Add Value

Cathy faced the reality that what she wanted in a new home she could not afford. She had been looking at three-bedroom homes in the suburbs with all the luxuries of "the rich and famous." She loved the idea of having a pool and a hot tub. She especially liked the workout room enclosed in glass. The large master bedroom with piped-in music, skylight in the bathroom, wraparound deck, and central vacuum system — all were what she wanted. The price tag on this gem was out of sight. She gave up her dream house and chose a modest-priced basic house on a half acre lot closer to the city limits. How could Cathy get her dream house?

Cathy needs to start thinking about the special features in a house that increase its value. She has made a wise decision in buying a smaller house on a large lot. Over the years, she can add special features to her home. She might put a deck on her home or enclose a porch. In time, as her home increases in value, she can decide whether to put more money into her home or sell it and move up to a higher-priced home with added features.

SPECIAL FEATURES

Generally, the special features that bring back far more value than the cost of their addition are:

- Upgraded kitchen
- Upgraded bathroom
- Additional bedroom or other living space
- Central air conditioning
- Energy efficient windows

- Naturally finished hardwood floors
- Quality carpeting
- Decks
- Screened porch
- Landscaping

Of more questionable value when deciding what special features you want to add to your home are items such as hot tubs and whirlpools, swimming pools, saunas, and steam rooms. These features can be standard in Hollywood mansions, in parts of California, at mountain resorts in Colorado and New England, or in the warmer climates of the South, and in parts of Florida. The weather has a major role to play regarding pools and spas. Resort areas are more influenced by the tourists they serve and are more likely to offer features like hot tubs and saunas. But in most homes, the liability and upkeep of in-ground or above-ground pools or the foreignness of saunas make these items of interest to only a few selective buyers.

LITTLE THINGS MEAN A LOT

Consider as you look for the house you want to buy, that if it only needs what is commonly referred to as cosmetic work — paint, wallpaper, etc. — you have the chance to add significant value to your property by adding some special features like decks and landscaping at a modest cost to you.

Upgraded Kitchen

The kitchen is one of the most important rooms in your house. An old house with an old kitchen will sell for much less than an old house with an upgraded kitchen. The price difference can be substantial. You can upgrade a kitchen on your own or with a contractor. New wood cabinets instead of old painted ones, a new counter top, some fresh wallpaper and light fixtures, a double sink, modern appliances, and new flooring will not only bring more enjoyment to you when you are in the kitchen, but they can bring more value to your home. Do not wait until you are ready to sell your house to upgrade the kitchen. A great deal of your time will be spent in this room alone or with your friends.

Upgraded Bathroom

The bathroom is another important room in the house that, with the addition of a few special features, will enhance the value of your home. A new vanity, sink, and medicine cabinet will do wonders for an old bathroom. A matching toilet, new flooring or carpet, and fresh paint or vinyl wall covering will make this a pleasant room in your home. You will very likely need a plumber to help with this project. On the other hand, if you are handy, this is a fun job with great rewards.

Measure the space you have to work in and then keep your eyes open for good prices on vanities, cabinets, toilets, and flooring. The cost of the upgrade will be well under the value it adds to your home.

Additional Living Space

Adding a bedroom or other living space to your home, especially if it has only two bedrooms, can add significant value and utility to your home. If the house has an attic, it may be possible to add a bedroom or study in that space. If you can add a bedroom and bath, even better. Get a contractor's advice before attempting remodeling of this nature, as it will generally involve running wiring, ductwork, and other systems into the space. Adding this additional living space could potentially add thousands to the value of your home.

Central Air Conditioning

Most people look for central air conditioning in a home in any area of the United States that has hot, humid summers or hot, dry weather. If the house has a heat pump, it has a dual capability that offers air conditioning. Many homes have window air conditioners. Given a choice between the hum of window air conditioners and the silent evenness and efficiency of central air conditioning, the latter is much preferred. It also adds more value to your home. Central air conditioning can be a costly addition, but one of lasting value, particularly if most homes in your area already have it.

Energy Efficient Windows

Energy efficient windows are valuable for several reasons. They add a dimension of insulation against cold winter winds, and they are easy to care for. Your home will be cooler in summer and warmer in winter. Styles are available to complement any style of home. Usually these windows are available in metal with a baked-on finish in limited colors or in white vinyl. They add a finished look to the house and value to your home.

Naturally Finished Hardwood Floors

Beautiful hardwood floors will bring compliments and value to your home. Many homes with beautifully finished wood floors incorporate area rugs as accents and to protect high traffic areas.

Refinishing hardwood floors is a tricky job. Don't attempt it on your own unless you have done it before. You could end up with dips and gouges in the floor if you are not careful.

Quality Carpeting

Walking on new soft carpet gives a feeling of comfort and a sense of warmth to your home. Carpeting helps to insulate and softens noises. Stain-resistant carpeting is a must for pet owners or for heavy traffic areas. It is possible for you to lay your own carpets, but I recommend getting an experienced carpet person to help you or to do the job for you. Wall-to-wall carpeting is a tough job to do well. Area rubber-backed carpets or recreation room indoor-outdoor carpet is easier to do on your own. Be sure to measure correctly and have the tools you need to cut and secure the carpet.

The addition of fresh new carpeting adds value to your home. Try to avoid outrageous or fad colors. You may tire of them or find that they are a drawback when you go to sell. Earth tones are always a good choice.

Decks

Decks can be added to your house in a number of ways. Pressure-treated wood is used for long-lasting wear. Some decks have built-in seats, some have decorative railings, some are natural wood, and some are stained. Decks can be built out from the ground floor, over a patio, garage, or roof, or out from a first or second floor sliding door. The floor plan of a deck can be tailored to suit whatever space is available. Decks can be layered from one level to another as they wrap around an area planned for outdoor living.

If you are handy, you can build the deck on your own or with the help of friends. Be sure to check on whether the wood should be treated to keep it from aging too quickly. If you decide to have a deck built for you, be sure to get two or three estimates. Have a plan and know the size deck you want. Check the other work the contractor has done in the area. Get in writing the total contract costs and timeline to complete the deck.

A deck is a special feature that brings great pleasure and adds value to your property too.

Screened Porch

Adding screening to an open outdoor porch at your house is another project you can do on your own or with friends who are handy. This special feature adds bug-free enjoyment to summer hours on the porch eating breakfast, playing cards with friends, or just reading. A few comfortable chairs and a table or two will make this a favorite area to spend some relaxing hours.

Landscaping

With a little imagination, a visit to the local nursery, and a magazine or two on gardening, you will be able to add color and charm to your home. Shrubs, flowering trees, and perennials give your home a finished look. Even something as simple as a patio table with an umbrella adds a festive and homey touch to your house.

Decide on areas for vegetable gardens, annual flowers, and perennials. Buy a few perennials each year. Check end of season sales, and you can get some plants at less than a quarter their normal cost.

If the landscaping around your house has been neglected and looks like a jungle of wild vines and weeds, get out the trimmers and groom the vegetation. You will be surprised and pleased with the results. The natural look may be fine, but if visitors have to fight their way past an overgrown hedge or bush, they may limit their visits.

OTHER SPECIALTY FEATURES

Hot Tub

There are many styles and sizes of hot tubs for you to choose from these days. Just go to any home builders' show in your area, and you will have the pick of the crop from two-person hot tubs to family-sized. They have different numbers of jet streams and massage streams. The molding for body contour varies, and you should sit in the tub as you would a car to assess its fit for you. Prices vary with the size and features offered. Although a hot tub will need care, most will be well worth the effort. Sometimes a warm bubbling dip will be just what you need to relax.

Before buying one, ask yourself about the location you have available for it. Will it be inside or outside of the house? Will it have privacy? Will tree leaves and debris get into it? Will it cause moisture problems if it is inside? What will be the cost of running it some of the year or year round? Are friends invited to use it? Will it remain clean or become a constant chore?

Swimming Pools

Although a rare find, the advantage of an indoor pool is year-round swimming in areas of the country with widely varying seasonal weather changes. A pool demands a lot of attention. The water must be treated to control bacteria and filtered for debris. Heated water is a plus, but it must be evenly heated for optimum enjoyment. Homes with a pool, indoor or outdoor, will need to be sure that their insurance covers accidents of family members or guests. Outdoor pools need to be fenced. Pool parties can be a great form of entertainment for the single person.

An above-ground pool is relatively easy to install because the land does not have to be excavated before the pool is set up. It is built on an above-ground frame, with steps to its walkway and pool. In most parts of the country, it is required that a safety fence be built around the pool to avoid accidental access by children, pets, and wild animals. A cover over the opening of the pool when not in use is always wise. Again, the pool water must be treated and kept clean. Prices vary as do sizes and space needed for installation.

Sauna

You could build a sauna if you had a space for it in your house. Some people especially enjoy dry heat. The sauna room can be designed to accommodate different numbers of people. Some saunas have lava rock to help maintain the even heat in the cabinet. Most have timers, and all will need a separate electrical line. Look at a wide variety of styles and sizes before you decide. Prices and craftsmen vary.

Steam Room

Some people prefer moist, vapor heat. It is rare to find a steam room in a personal residence. It is far more common to go to a health club for this type of relaxation. If you want to install a steam room in your house, you will need a plumber and an appro-priate place to install the room. Costs of installation vary.

ITEMS TO REMEMBER

As you proceed with your house hunting, keep in mind that a property that needs some cosmetic work or that can be upgraded is a property with potential for increased value. It may be well worth the time and effort you will spend on it. In the long run, you may very well be able to sell this house one day for a profit and move ever closer to your dream house!

QUICK CHECKLIST SPECIAL FEATURES

1. Does the property that you are looking at have a place for a deck to be added?

2. Does it have an open porch? Can it be screened?

3. Is the landscaping wild and ungroomed? Does it need work?

4. Is the kitchen old-fashioned and in need of an upgrade?

5. Does the house have carpeting? Does it need replacement?

6. Is the bathroom old-fashioned and in need of an upgrade?

7. Are the floors covered or natural wood? Are they in good condition? Would you consider finishing them?

8. Does the house have window air conditioners or does it have central air conditioning?

9. Are there storm and screen windows on the house? Would new energy efficient windows be of added benefit?

10. Is there potential for additional living space?

11. Can you do most of the cosmetic work that needs to be done?

— 17 —
Landlording

Randy was looking for a house with an apartment in it so that he could rent it out to offset his mortgage payment. As he looked, he found that these properties were more expensive than he had expected. However, he found one that he could afford with a tenant already living in the apartment. He thought that this would be perfect. The property was in excellent condition and would not need any work before he could move in. He paid top dollar for it. He realized that the tenant was not paying enough rent and thought that he would adjust it soon. He also thought it would be a good idea to separate the heat and electric bills from the house to the apartment, which had not been done over the years. At settlement, he had received the security deposit and had noticed that the tenant had a month-to-month informal handwritten lease. The month after settlement, the tenant moved out and told him to apply the security deposit to the last month's rent, which he had not received. What was Randy learning about being a landlord?

Randy will be more careful from now on. He will be sure to have a formal lease. He will make it clear that a security deposit is not rent. He will be sure to adjust the rent to cover upkeep and repair for the apartment. He will be prepared for the burden of a vacancy on his monthly payments. He will be sure to check the cost of separating heat and electricity to the apartment. The next time Randy considers buying a multi-unit house, he will know to look out for these problems.

MULTI-FAMILY DWELLINGS

Buying a multi-family dwelling of two to four units is procedurally similar to purchasing a single family dwelling. You will probably pay more for a multi-family dwelling, but it will also have the potential to earn more in the long run.

Consider that you will live in one of the two-bedroom units and rent out the other unit(s). Depending on the size of the other units, you will be able to rent them at the going rate in your area. Keep in mind that each unit should have a separate electric meter and heating if at all possible. Water service and sewer will more than likely be billed to you. You will need to take those expenses along with taxes, insurance, and repairs into consideration, total them for the year, divide by twelve, and establish a margin of profit before you set the rent rates for each unit.

You will want to avoid a negative cash flow whenever possible. By that I mean that your monthly rental income should equal or exceed your monthly payments and expenses.

WHAT DO LANDLORDS DO?

As a landlord, you will have to keep meticulous records. Equally important will be your interest in working with all types of people: tenants, workers, service providers, and officials. You must be prepared to receive telephone calls at all hours from tenants reporting noise, leaks, broken appliances, bugs, and so on. You will need to refresh an apartment for your new tenant with paint and clean bathrooms and kitchens. This changeover usually takes place at the end of a month on a weekend. If you do not have the time or the energy or the knowhow, you will have to hire someone to do it for you.

Keep in mind that you will be responsible for:
- Advertising the apartment
- Selecting the tenants
- Setting the rent rate
- Preparing the lease
- Setting the rules
- Providing prompt service and repairs
- Keeping meticulous records of income and expenses

Advertising the Apartment
There are many ways to advertise your apartment. You can place an ad in the local newspaper. You can put a sign in the window of the apartment. You can tell friends and ask to put signs up on a church or health club bulletin board.

Describing the apartment in desirable terms will help draw attention to your ad. For example:

> One-bedroom apartment in Historic District overlooking river. No pets. $500 monthly plus utilities. Call for appointment. (123) 555-1234

Selecting the Tenant
You should have an application for the prospective tenant to fill out. You can either make one up on your computer or typewriter or buy a prepared example at an office supply store. You will need the tenant's permission to verify the information with his or her current employer and previous landlord. Screening this information is very important. If you are satisfied with the references and your interview with the prospective tenant, take a deposit, which can be a half or full month's rent or more, and

prepare the lease with the terms agreed upon. Establish the rent and other responsibilities with the applicant. There should be no surprises for the tenant when he or she meets with you to sign the lease and get the keys.

Set the Rent
Be familiar with the rental rates in your neighborhood for the size and condition of your apartment. The part of the country you live in will dictate the level of rental rates. Some cities, for example, have "rent control," while others do not. An apartment in a house in a desirable residential neighborhood may bring a higher rent than apartment buildings in marginal neighborhoods. Historic district apartments may bring higher rent because of the desire of some people to live in these areas of distinction.

Prepare the Lease
The lease is a legal document between you, the landlord, and the tenant. It is important and should be filled out carefully. You can buy a standard lease at an office supply store. This is your opportunity to specify the conditions of your rental agreement for the apartment with the tenant. Special clauses state extra items to the standard lease agreement, such as cutting the grass, shoveling snow, restrictions or agreements regarding pets, number of people permitted to occupy the apartment, penalties for late rent payments, tenant responsibility for minor maintenance, such as changing light bulbs.

The lease specifies the dates for the term of the lease, the procedures for renewal or termination, and those named on the lease who are responsible for carrying out the agreement. All parties responsible for the terms of the lease will sign and so will the landlord. It will be dated and is a legally binding document. Both the tenant and the landlord get a copy of the signed lease.

Set Up the Rules
Remember that this is your property. The tenants are paying guests and will be asked to follow your wishes in the form of rules. For example, your rules might include the following:

- Security lights should be on at night.
- Main entrances should be locked and secure for the safety of tenants.
- Loud music and parties are not permitted after 10 p.m.
- Trash and garbage must be placed in assigned containers.

Rules are designed to protect the safety and well-being of everyone living in rather close proximity. People want a pleasant place to live with minimal hassles.

Provide Prompt Service and Repairs

It is said that high vacancy rates indicate poor service and lack of needed repairs. Your tenants expect to have functioning plumbing and heating, a working refrigerator and stove, hall lights and outdoor lights at the door. In addition, in some localities, if you do not provide these minimum services, your tenant may legally withhold rent payments until they are fixed.

Remember that unattended water leaks will eventually cost you more than you will want to pay. Water may stain ceilings and wallpaper or even cause ceilings to fall. Fixing minor problems early is always a good idea to prevent escalating problems. Electrical service, needless to say, is critical to a well-maintained apartment and its safety.

It is always important to have reliable service people available and willing to work on these projects for you if you are unable to do the work yourself. You should have names of at least three plumbers and electricians who provide twenty-four hour service.

Keep Meticulous Records

If record keeping is a problem for you now, it will be a nightmare for you with added apartments. Develop a system of forms to help you get organized in this task of record keeping. It is very important that your records of income and expenses be in order for tax and budgeting purposes. You will need to know what your monthly cash flow is; in other words, you will need to know what you earn and what you spend on each apartment. The whole idea of owning a multi-family dwelling is to offset your costs and, in time, to make a profit. If the property is showing a negative cash flow over an extended period of time, you are losing too much money and need to correct the negative flow as soon as possible.

It is a good idea to make up some forms or buy some standard forms for the necessary record keeping you will be doing. For example:

- Monthly operating statement
- Purchase orders
- Resident ledger
- Rental application and verification form
- Deposit receipt
- Notice to vacate
- Notice to pay rent or vacate

Monthly Operating Statement. This form would include information on the specific rental property's monthly income, deposits, and expenses. The best way to itemize expenses is to put them into categories. Common groupings could be:

- Expenses:
    Utilities
    Cleaning
    Insurance
    Taxes
    Advertising
    Repairs and Supplies
    Pest Control
    Miscellaneous

- Resident Manager's Expenses (if you have a manager)
- Capital Improvements:
    Carpet Replacement
    Window Shades or Drape Replacement
    Painting
    Roofing
    Water Heater Replacement
- Investment Expenses include:
    Accounting
    Legal
    Professional Property Management

Purchase Order Forms. These forms are very useful in keeping track of the supplies you purchase. These forms will give you a record of expenses. For example, if you purchase door locks, window shades, paint, and light bulbs, you can use a purchase order for your records. Generally, the form should include the following information:

- Date
- Order number
- Supplier
- Quantity
- Description of item
- Price paid
- Date received

Resident's Ledger. This is a record for each individual apartment. It is a quick look at the history of a tenant's record of payment while living in the apartment. This form could have the following information on it:

- Tenant's name
- Telephone number
- Apartment number
- Person to contact in an emergency
- Employer with telephone number
- Lease date (from ____ to ____)
- Rental rate per month
- Security deposit and other deposits
- Rental rate changes
- Date of payments

Rental Application and Verification Form. This form is very useful for you to use when selecting tenants. The information you could gather on this form might include:

- Name
- Date of birth
- Social Security number
- Names of children
- Children's dates of birth
- Pets
- Marital status

- Present address, telephone number
- Present landlord, telephone number
- Previous landlord, telephone number
- Driver's license number
- Automobile, make, year, license number
- Person to contact in emergency
- Employment (present and previous)
- Occupation and gross monthly income
- Welfare and unemployment history
- Credit/banking (three sources with telephone numbers)

Deposit Receipt. This is a statement you can use to clarify the terms for the deposit the tenant gives you on the apartment. It should acknowledge that you have received a specific sum which is non-interest bearing and not a rental payment. It should state that the deposit will be refunded fourteen days after the tenant vacates, provided the premises are in good condition. It should also state that the owner will refund the deposit in full if the applicant is not approved. In some states, deposit money put in escrow will earn interest after a tenant has resided in the apartment for three years or longer.

Notice to Vacate. This is the usual way a tenant informs you that he wishes to vacate the apartment. The usual thirty-day notice to vacate is common in most states. You will be free to show the apartment to prospective tenants by appointment.

Notice to Pay Rent or Vacate. This is a form you hope to use very rarely. It informs the tenant that unless rent is paid by a specific date, he must move out. If he fails to pay or move by the date specified, you may begin eviction procedures.

Being a landlord is challenging. Be sure that you understand your legal rights. Be sure that you understand the tenant's legal rights. Talk with your lawyer so that you will be well advised as you enter the multi-family dwelling business. Each state has its own statutes to protect tenants and landlords. Become familiar with your laws. In addition to a lawyer, have a good accountant who is able to guide you in your record keeping and major expenditure decisions.

If you enjoy meeting many types of people and can make wise decisions, being a landlord can be enjoyable and profitable.

QUICK CHECKLIST
LANDLORDING

1. Will you live in one of the units?
2. Will the income exceed the expenses?
3. Do you have a record keeping system?
4. Do you have a tenant application form?
5. Do you have a lease ready to use?
6. Will you be able to provide prompt service and repairs when needed?
7. Have you asked your lawyer for information on your state's statutes regarding tenant's rights and responsibilities?
8. Have you asked your lawyer for information on your state's statutes regarding landlord's rights and responsibilities?
9. Are you prepared for telephone calls from tenants at all hours?
10. How will you advertise your vacancies?

Glossary

ACCEPTANCE — Voluntarily agreeing to the price and terms of an offer. The offer and acceptance create a contract.

ADJUSTABLE RATE MORTGAGE (ARM) — Mortgage loan under which the interest rate is periodically adjusted to coincide more closely with current rates. The amounts and times of adjustment are agreed to at the inception of the loan.

AGREEMENT OF SALE — Has two separate meanings, depending on area of the country. In some states, it is synonymous with a purchase agreement. In other states, it is synonymous with a land contract.

AMORTIZATION — Payment of a debt in equal installments of principal and interest, as opposed to interest only payments.

ANNUAL PERCENTAGE RATE (APR) — The yearly interest percentage of a loan, as expressed by the actual rate of interest paid. The APR is disclosed as a requirement of federal truth-in-lending statutes.

APPRAISAL — An opinion of value based upon a factual analysis. Legally, an estimation of value by two disinterested persons of suitable qualifications.

APPROVED ATTORNEY — In states where attorneys examine the chain of title before title insurance is issued, the title company will approve certain attorneys as those whose opinion it will accept for the issuance of a title policy.

"AS IS" CONDITION — Premises accepted by a buyer or tenant in the condition existing at the time of the sale or lease, including all physical defects.

ASKING PRICE — The price at which the seller is offering property for sale. The eventual selling price may be less after negotiation with a buyer.

ASSESSMENT — (1) The estimating of value of property for tax purposes. (2) A levy against property in addition to general taxes. Usually for improvements such as streets, sewers, etc.

ASSETS — Everything owned by a person that can be used for the payment of debts.

ASSUMPTION OF MORTGAGE — Agreement by a buyer to assume the liability under an existing note secured by a mortgage or deed of trust. The lender usually must approve the new debtor in order to release the existing debtor (usually the seller) from liability.

BALLOON NOTE — A note calling for periodic payments, which are sufficient to fully amortize the face amount of the note prior to maturity, so that a principal sum known as a "balloon" is due at maturity.

BENEFICIARY — (1) One for whose benefit a trust is created. (2) In states in which deeds of trust are commonly used instead of mortgages, the lender (mortgagee) is called the beneficiary.

BREACH OF CONTRACT — Failure to perform a contract, in whole or part, without legal excuse.

CASHIER'S CHECK — A check drawn by a bank on itself rather than on an account of a depositor. A cashier's check is generally acceptable to close a sale without waiting for the check to clear.

CERTIFICATE OF SALE — Certificate issued to the buyer at a judicial sale (such as a tax sale), which will entitle the buyer to a deed upon confirming of the sale by the court or if the land is not redeemed within a specified time.

CIRCUIT BREAKER — An electrical device that has taken the place of the fuse in most homes. The circuit is broken (electricity shut off) when there is an overload. The circuit breaker can be reset rather than replaced as a fuse must be.

CLOSING — In real estate sales, the final procedure in which documents are executed (signed) and/or recorded and the sale (or loan) is completed.

CLOUD ON TITLE — An invalid encumbrance on real property, which, if valid, would affect the rights of the owner. The cloud may be removed by quitclaim deed, or, if necessary, by court action.

COMMISSION — An amount, usually a percentage, paid to an agent (real estate broker) as compensation for services. The amount to a real estate broker is generally a percentage of the sale price or total rental.

COMMITMENT — A written promise to make or insure a loan for a specific amount and on specific terms.

CONTRACT OF SALE — In some areas of the country, synonymous with land contract. In other areas, synonymous with purchase agreement.

CONVENTIONAL MORTGAGE (LOAN) — A mortgage or deed of trust not obtained under a government-insured program such as FHA or VA.

CREDIT — The financial worthiness of a borrower. The history of whether this borrower has met financial obligations on time in the past.

DEED — Any one of many conveyancing or financing instruments, but generally a conveyancing instrument, given to pass fee title to property upon sale.

DEED OF TRUST — An instrument used in many states in place of a mortgage. Property is transferred to a trustee by the borrower (trustor), in favor of the lender (beneficiary), and reconveyed upon payment in full.

DEPOSIT — Money given by the buyer with an offer to purchase. Shows good faith. Also called earnest money.

EQUITY — The market value of real estate, less the amount of existing liens.

ESCROW ACCOUNT — Account held by a lender for payment of taxes, insurance, or other periodic debts against real property. The borrower pays a portion with each monthly payment, and the lender pays the tax bill from the accumulated funds.

FAIR MARKET VALUE — Price that probably would be negotiated between a willing seller and willing buyer in a reasonable time. Usually arrived at by comparable sales in the area.

FEDERAL HOUSING LAW — Title VIII of the Civil Rights Act, which forbids discrimination in the sale or rental of residential property because of race, color, sex, religion, or national origin.

FEE SIMPLE — Commonly a synonym for ownership.

FULL DISCLOSURE — In real estate, revealing all the known facts that may affect the decision of a buyer or tenant. A broker must disclose known defects in the property for sale or lease. A broker cannot charge a commission to a buyer and seller unless both know and agree.

G.I. LOAN — See Veterans Administration (VA) Loan.

GOOD FAITH — Something done with good intentions, without knowledge of fraudulent circumstances or reason to inquire further.

INTEREST RATE — The percentage of an amount of money that is paid for its use for a specified time. Usually expressed as an annual percentage.

INTESTATE — Without leaving a will, or leaving an invalid will so that the property of the estate passes by the laws of succession rather than by direction of the deceased.

LEASE WITH OPTION TO PURCHASE — A lease under which the lessee has the right to purchase the property. The price and terms of the purchase must be set forth for the option to be valid.

MARKET VALUE — The highest price a willing buyer would pay and a willing seller accept, both being fully informed, and the property exposed for a reasonable period of time.

MORTGAGE — To hypothecate (pledge to another) as security, real property for the payment of a debt. The borrower retains possession and use of the property.

OFFER — A presentation or proposal for acceptance, in order to form a contract. To be legally binding, an offer must be definite as to price and terms.

OWNERSHIP — Rights to the use, enjoyment, and alienation of property, to the exclusion of others.

PLANNING COMMISSION — A board of a city, county, or similar local government, which must approve proposed building projects. Often must be confirmed by a higher board, such as a council.

PROPERTY TAX — Generally, a tax levied on both real and personal property; the amount of the tax is dependent on the value of the property.

QUITCLAIM DEED — A deed operating as a release; intended to pass any title, interest, or claim the grantor may have in the property, but not containing any warranty of a valid interest or title in the grantor.

RATE INDEX — An index used to adjust the interest rate of an adjustable mortgage loan.

RECORDING — Filing documents affecting real property as a matter of public record, giving notice to future purchasers, creditors, or other interested parties. Recording is controlled by statutes and usually requires the witnessing and notarizing of an instrument to be recorded.

REPAIRS — The general upkeep of property without major replacement or change of the plan or characteristics of the building.

RESTRICTION — Most commonly used to describe a use or uses prohibited to the owner of land. Restrictions are set forth by former owners in deeds or in a declaration of restrictions recorded by a developer.

RIGHT OF WAY — The right itself to pass over the land of another, in this case to reach your property.

SETTLEMENT STATEMENT — A statement prepared by a broker or lender, giving a complete breakdown of costs involved in a real estate sale. Separate statements are prepared for the seller and buyer.

TITLE INSURANCE — Insurance against loss resulting from defects of title to a specific described parcel of real property.

UNENCUMBERED — Free of liens and other encumbrances. Free and clear.

WILL — A written expression of the desire of a person as to the deposition of that person's property after death. Must follow certain procedures to be valid.

ZONING — The division of a city or county by legislative regulations into areas (zones), specifying the uses allowable for the real property in these areas.

ZONING ORDINANCE — A limitation on use of the property by law.

Reprinted in part from PUB. No. 510, *The Real Estate Dictionary*, Copyright 1992 Financial Publication Co., 82 Brookline Ave., Boston, MA 02215

References

Bellairs, Herbert; Helsel, James; Caldwell, Thomas. *Modern Real Estate Practice in Pennsylvania*, 4th Edition. Chicago: Real Estate Education Company, 1986.

Bellairs, Herbert; Helsel, James; Poorman, George. *Modern Real Estate Practice in Pennsylvania*, 2nd Edition. Chicago: Real Estate Education Company, 1978.

Bix, Cynthia Overbeck. *Home Repair Handbook*, 9th Printing. Menlo Park, CA.: Sunset Publishing Corporation, 1992.

Branson, Gary D. *The Complete Guide to Remodeling Your Basement*. White Hall, VA: Betterway Publications, Inc., 1990.

Bridges, J.E.; Bridges, D.S. *Mortgage Loans, What's Right For You*. 2nd Edition. White Hall, VA: Betterway Publications, Inc., 1989.

Granfield, Mary. "Sweet Toxic Home." *Money*. June, 1992:130.

Greater Harrisburg Association of Realtors. Forms. Harrisburg, PA. 1992.

Luts, Jack; Peterson, Pete. *The Complete Guide to Painting Your Home*. White Hall, VA: Betterway Publications, Inc., 1989.

Madorma, James. *The Complete Guide to Understanding and Caring for Your Home*. White Hall, VA: Betterway Publications, Inc., 1991.

——. *The Home Buyer's Inspection Guide*. White Hall, VA: Betterway Publications, Inc., 1990.

Publication 510, *The Real Estate Dictionary*. Boston: Financial Publishing Co., 1992.

Wood, P. Nicholson. *Ladner on Conveyancing in Pennsylvania*, 3rd Edition. Philadelphia: George T. Bisel Co., 1961.

Woodson, R. Dodge. *The Complete Guide to Buying Your First Home*. White Hall, VA: Betterway Publications, Inc., 1992.

Index

About the Author

Elaine J. Anderson, Ph.D., has been a teacher in high school and college, an administrator and a business owner. She is currently on the faculty of Education at Bloomsburg University of Pennsylvania. She has bought, sold, and managed her own rental properties and renovated properties in the Historic District of Harrisburg, PA for many years. She has a Realtor's license in Pennsylvania, is a single home buyer, and is a partner in the ownership of a home.